WEB**ANIMATION**

START HERE!

ALL THAT YOU NEED TO CREATE YOUR
OWN FANTASTIC WEB ANIMATIONS

GRAHAM DAVIS

I L E X

CONTENTS

Introduction

You may have seen animation featured on general websites, or even surfed onto some of the fantastic sites dedicated to pushing back the boundaries of animation techniques. If you thought, 'I want to do some of that', then *Web Animation: Start Here!* is the book for you. The exercises over the following chapters will enable you to create great animations within hours, rather than months. Like most creative people, you'll probably want to run before you can walk, but you will make quicker and more genuine progress if you follow the projects through in sequence. We've created them so that key concepts are introduced at the right time; and if you follow all the steps, you will quickly develop new skills and build on them until you have a good grounding in the basics you'll need to compete with the experts. So what do you need to become a Web animator? Well, the essentials are ideas, software and webspace.

Ideas

Where do great ideas come from? Almost every great animator began by copying other people's work. This is no bad thing: if you do this as well, you will learn from the greats, while gradually developing your own 'voice' – that mix of original ideas and distinctive style which will get you noticed. The Web is full of inspiration, and you can find some links at *www.webanimation.web-linked.com*.

Also, think about a TV show like *The Simpsons*, which attracts huge, worldwide audiences. It's a global success, but uses a simple, two-dimensional (2D) technique and bright, primary colours. What it also does, though, is rely on great storylines and distinctive characters for its appeal. If nothing else, this demonstrates what you can achieve with imagination, observation and original material. Your own ambitions may be more modest; you might simply want some animated graphics for your homepage, for example. But whatever the scale of your ambition, *Web Animation: Start Here!* has some ideas for you to try out – and you will also be shown how to integrate them with your website.

Software

You will almost certainly be creating your animation on a PC or Mac. Fortunately, all the main software applications are available on both platforms, and once your animation is uploaded to the Web it can be viewed by everyone. In each project, we'll say which software *we've* used to create the examples, but also suggest some suitable alternatives. We all know that software can be expensive, but many suppliers allow you to download a trial version of their product, which is usually 'save disabled' or time-limited to 30 days. In addition, there is a wide range of shareware available – see *www.webanimation.web-linked.com* for links. Shareware is usually distributed so that the user pays a modest fee if they wish to use it beyond 30 days, but sometimes it's totally free.

Webspace

Webspace is usually affordable, and in some parts of the world, is available free from many service providers. The Web is a fantastic showcase for the animator's craft, since it provides a potential worldwide audience (if you can tell the online community where to find your work!). Modern software has also removed many of the barriers that existed when animation was largely created with drawings, cells, rostrum cameras and film.

Despite this, you will find one limitation online: bandwidth. What's this? Well, imagine having to pour milk onto your breakfast cereal using a straw. The Web is not so different: it is a mass of small 'pipes' (the existing communications networks) through which ever-greater numbers of people are pushing more and more data. That's why, for many people with slow, dial-up connections, the Internet experience can be a frustrating one of slow download times and other problems. But higher speed connections (i.e. bigger pipes), such as ISDN, ADSL and cable modems mean that the long wait for animations to download will soon diminish. In the meantime, however, it is sensible to create animations that are of a relatively small file size. Remember: you should avoid creating animations for people with fast connections, when the vast majority of your audience won't have them yet. Our projects will show you how to do this without spoiling your work.

Of course, 2D animation is primarily the art of illusion – the illusion of movement and perspective. For example, in the project on page 104, the woman appears from the distance, enters the building through the arch and moves into the foreground. Similarly, the figure in the project on page 131 *appears* to travel past the background scene; but in fact it's the background that moves. Most of the techniques to achieve this illusion of movement are fairly easy to learn and you will be taught them as you work through the book.

That said, in the simplest form of Web animation, objects do literally move. A Web design package capable of creating DHTML (Dynamic HTML – see Glossary) is all you need to create movement. The objects that can be animated in this way are many and varied: text, graphic objects, scanned images, traced bitmaps converted to vectors, digital photos and video grabs, or original images created in vector and bitmap applications. The only constraint is that they must first be converted to one of the standard Web image file formats. And if you don't know the difference between vector and bitmap images, then be sure to read page 14 carefully.

To the novice, the Web can seem a bewildering place. To make life simpler, the things you need to know have been separated from the things you might *like* to know. So, if you want to find out more about Shockwave, QuickTime, RealVideo, Windows Media Player, SVG, VRML, 3D, plug-ins, etc, then refer to the Glossary and all will be revealed. To make your life easier still, the three primary animation technologies have been used to create all of the projects in the book: DHTML, Animated GIF and Flash.

But first the basics: to view any webpage you need a browser, which normally comes preinstalled on a PC or Mac. Browsers convert the invisible code (HTML) that underlies every webpage into the text you see onscreen, and in most cases import the accompanying images. With DHTML, though, an animation starts at point A and, for example, 15 frames later (or one second) arrives at point B; it's that simple. DHTML animation can extend across an entire webpage, while GIF animation appears within a smaller, self-contained box. Each frame of a GIF animation has to be created as a separate bitmap image. GIF animation is the oldest Web animation format, but is still popular. *Web Animation: Start Here!* shows you how to get the most out of it.

But the most versatile Web animation format is Macromedia's Flash. The animations you most admire online were probably created using it. The Flash player started life as a browser plug-in, but recent browsers come supplied with it pre-installed. Flash is timeline-based vector animation (although it handles bitmaps equally well). If all your animation is vector-based (see Glossary), then it can be scaled up or down in size by simply dragging the browser window. The image quality will remain the same.

To complete the projects, you obviously need a PC or Mac as well as software (applications) to assemble or create DHTML, Animated GIF or Flash animations, and other packages for vector drawing and bitmap editing. A scanner would also be useful. And if you are inspired to move on to 3D animation, then you will need all the 'horsepower' in your hardware that you can afford!

PART 1

The 2D Illusion

The Web opens up the whole world to prospective animators. Now anyone can create an animation and put it on show using public webspace. The abundance and variety of animation online is truly mind-blowing. Even on nonspecialist, general websites you might find animated buttons, avant-garde graphics, humble banner ads, cartoons, e-mail greeting cards, Web navigation systems, animated diagrams and much, much more. There is extensive crossover between these areas too, which makes the future of Web animation both exciting and unpredictable. But one feature is common to all: finding a way to suggest and manage movement.

10 MOVEMENT AND SPACE

The simplest form of Web animation is moving a single object across a space. For example, a balloon ascending skywards, or a cartoon Pteradon plummeting towards the ground (see the frame illustrated opposite).

Hingeing, pivoting and rotating are all simple forms too, since they comprise a mainly static image that has one or two moving parts. Take the second illustrated example on this page: in the word 'TRAP', the crossbar of the 'A' drops down like a trapdoor, then snaps shut having captured a wandering fly. Look at our website (see page 6).

The next stage is an object that travels across a space while it is itself changing. In the third example illustrated opposite, an 'f' absentmindedly struggles to catch up with 'orgot' and form a complete word.

A further technique, morphing, describes the process of a stationary object changing into another object entirely, such as a square becoming a circle, the word 'Hunter' becoming the word 'Hunted', or a heart swelling (see the fourth example opposite).

All the above examples share a common attribute: they exist in a 'flatland', where there is no attempt to imply the depth and perspective found in the physical world.

Movement and depth

Animation guru Richard Taylor describes the process of animation as not so much making drawings move, as drawing movement. So, once you have mastered the techniques of animating in flatland, you will probably want to add some 'depth' to your animation.

But before we move on, let's pause for a moment to examine 2D and 3D spaces. It should be readily apparent that 3D animation exists in a virtual 3D space on a monitor screen, which has x, y and z axes. In a 2D virtual space (think of *The Simpsons* again) the illusion of depth is created by putting objects onto layers, with the objects on the top layer obscuring those beneath. We use software to manipulate these layers, but in traditional cell animation there could be four or five transparent

1 *Moving words or images, the raw material of animation.*

2 *Gentle wit can be more effective than obvious humour.*

3 *The expected or unexpected can both have compelling results.*

4 *Nonverbal communication.*

cells stacked in layers, each with specific parts of the animation painted on them. In this way, only the part of the image that changed, a moving arm for example, required a cell change. Each individual frame was then copied to film. The whole process was (and remains) very laborious.

Layers also allow you to create a more convincing impression of movement, and there are a variety of techniques you can use to achieve this. When an object or character appears to travel while remaining in the centre of the screen, it is the background image that must be moved rather than the object itself. To achieve this, of course, the background image must be wider than the animation frame. This is called a Panning

5

6

7

8

9

5 *2D space animation can only suggest a 3D space.*

6 *A typical six-step walking sequence. In midstep, the figure rises slightly.*

7 *Multilayered 2D animation techniques owe their origin to traditional cell animation.*

8 *Each character moves forwards a small amount if the walking sequence is to be convincing.*

9 *Causing an object to hurtle towards a distant opening is a perspective technique that is often used.*

Background. A static figure would look unreal against it, so the figure needs to be partially animated using a 'walk on the spot' sequence.

An even more convincing technique to create depth and movement is to first make a static background in soft focus, and then add another layer in front of that containing a slightly out-of-focus panning background. On the layer above that you can place a figure walking on the spot and, finally, on a foreground layer in front of the figure, put some objects like lampposts or trees on a much wider panning background. The topmost panning layer moves faster than the panning layer behind the figure. This creates a very effective animation, akin to looking out of a car window and seeing the hedgerow rush past more quickly than the distant hills.

These techniques are just as effective when applied to graphic objects and text, and even to abstract shapes and colours. There will also be times when a figure walks across the screen, and for this a walking sequence is required. Picture 8 shows a typical example, which can be varied depending on the character's size and shape.

Finally we reach the outer limits of 2D animation: perspective movement. Imagine an object or figure appearing to come towards you or move away from from you. A classic example would be a train rushing towards you or a spacecraft coming from behind your head and zooming away into the distance. Picture 9 shows how this can be achieved by using a vector drawing application. Another classic variation is the view through a car windshield travelling down an endless highway. The car remains static as the movement comes from a sequence of background images with road markings and telephone poles in different positions. Graphic objects and text can also be animated using variations of this technique. The best ways to achieve such effects will be discussed throughout *Web Animation: Start Here!*.

1

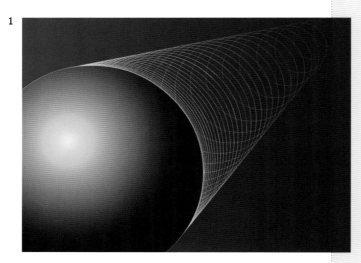

Speed

There is one more feature that will make animated movement more convincing, and that is the use of acceleration and deceleration – in other words, the control of speed. Remember the classic cartoon image of a figure skidding to a halt just before a cliff edge? In animation terms, when an object 'accelerates' it covers the same distance in increasingly fewer frames (or a greater number of frames when when it decelerates). Many animated actions require a variation in speed – the golf ball animation on page 92, for example. Flash has a fantastic feature for easily controlling acceleration and deceleration.

Style and character

Animation, like any visual art, evokes an emotional response in the viewer, so style is important even if your content consists of simple graphics.
For example, a graphic may be funky, retro, clean, hypnotic, cosy, avant-garde, frenetic, etc., and if it is figure-based, you can make your characters suggest any emotion. The examples opposite show how varied Web animation styles can be.

2

1 *This wireframe view shows the Flash acceleration feature. As the sphere gets further away it speeds up; each frame (ring) travels a progressively greater distance over the same time.*

2 *Here is a selection of images that are suitable for animating. They are all vector images, so they can be ungrouped and edited into new shapes or positions.*

Sound

Whether you use sound effects, voices or music, sound can enhance Web animation. However, it does add an extra level of complexity, so in this book we've limited the coverage of sound to effects, such as a door slamming, and to short sections of looped (repeated) music.

Sound files are readily available as free downloads: see *www.webanimation.web-linked.com* for links. Web animations with voiceovers or synchronised speech have to be converted to a format like QuickTime, so they can be downloaded to the browser in a stream (with the first portion playing while the second is downloading).

Backgrounds, layout and planning

The size and proportions of your Web animation will depend on how you plan to use it. This is discussed in detail in the next chapter. However, there are aesthetic considerations as well as practical ones. Professional Web animators, like their counterparts in film and TV, often start with a storyboard. In a Web context specifically, this allows them to experiment with different proportions; after all, a Web animation doesn't have to match a computer screen's ratio of 4:3, width to height; it can occupy any part of the screen. Using a storyboard, you can also indicate when a change of background occurs, and, if it is a panning background, how much wider than the frame it should be. If you become a professional Web animator, such a storyboard will form your initial presentation to a client.

Meanwhile, use storyboards to write yourself notes; this will help you to manage continuity in longer, multiscene animations – such as for the colour values of an animated object, for example.

14 PREPARING TO ANIMATE

You can animate anything, as long as it is saved in, or converted to, one of the standard Web image formats. But what other basics do you need to know before you start?

Colour

The Web uses the RGB (Red, Green, Blue) colour model; this is the same method used to display colours on your computer monitor. You should ensure that your vector and bitmap applications are set to this before you start. For some, RGB will be the default setting, while for others it may be CMYK or even PANTONE, which are designed for high-end print reproduction rather than the Web.

Before you start making animations, we should spend a moment looking at how an image is created on a computer. The two methods – bitmap and vector – are perhaps best demonstrated by the following example. First, imagine two rectangles in the centre of a white space, filled with a two-colour, graduated blend of blue and red. One rectangle has been created in a bitmap application, the other in vectors. Now imagine those two rectangles joined together to form a square (see picture 2 opposite).

Bitmap

If an image is a bitmap, it's as if a very fine invisible grid has been laid over it and each cell of the grid contains the digital values of the colours. With the colour blend in our example, each vertical row will be slightly different from the one above it and below it. All the information is recorded so that it can be displayed on a monitor, or sent to a printer. (This is how a scanner works too, recording the colour values of thousands of scan lines.) If a bitmap is enlarged, therefore, the pixels (cells) are enlarged, which means a loss of image quality.

Vector

A vector image is described entirely in text. The text for our example might be: 'image size 500 x 500 pixels, background colour white, draw

1

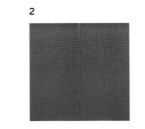

2

3

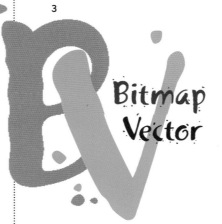

4

1 *The top row are the colours that are native to your computer monitor and will be used in the animations: RGB, or Red, Green and Blue. Below them are the four process colours that are used for printing: CMYK or Cyan, Magenta, Yellow and Key Plate (Black). Some animations at* **www.webexpertseries.com** *will have slightly different colours to the printed page, as certain RGB colours do not have CMYK equivalents.*

2 *The two halves of the image may look the same, but the left side is a rather poor bitmap, while the right side is a top of the class vector.*

3 *With an outline shape like a letterform, the bitmap (top) reveals nasty, jagged parts when enlarged, while the vector (below) scales perfectly.*

4 *The humble GIF; the left half saved in the maximum 256 colours, the right half saved in just 8 colours with a dither to compensate for the lack of colours.*

rectangle starting at a position 100 pixels down from top boundary, 100 pixels from left boundary, rectangle is 300 pixels wide, 300 pixels deep, fill rectangle with horizontal blend starting as blue finishing as red.' All this information is then recorded so that it can be displayed on a monitor.

The vector has a big advantage over bitmap, since it is scalable without any loss of quality. So what? Well, as you can see, the bitmap slavishly records everything, even though each white pixel is identical to the next, which results in a relatively large file size. The vector, however, cleverly avoids repetition – it's a bit like a gene, in that it records only the information required to reproduce itself.

So why do we bother with bitmaps at all? The problem with the vector image is that it can only be (re)created within a computer. If you want to use a photograph, however, you need to scan a print it or take it using a digital camera, but both operate exclusively in the bitmap domain.

How does all this technical stuff affect your Web animations? It all comes down to bandwidth. Bitmaps create larger files than vectors, so vectors display more quickly, avoiding that tiresome wait for a webpage to download. But a historical problem remains: the Internet was first conceived for scientists who wanted to share data with each other, 99 per cent of which was text. When consumer demand for online information and entertainment took off, the GIF (Graphics Interchange Format) appeared, to satisfy the need for images to make websites more attractive. However, GIF was conceived when your PC or Mac would have been running at 16MHz, your modem at 9600 and your 13 or 14-in monitor was unlikely to display more than 256 colours. So GIF was designed to recognize these limitations, reducing the image to just 256 discrete colours rather than the 16.7 million we currently enjoy.
It was also compressed, so that it could travel faster down the very narrow 'pipework' and be decompressed by the browser for final display onscreen. Soon afterwards the animated GIF appeared, so the Web was a effectively a vector-free zone.

Nowadays things have changed and we can use vector images on the Web in the form of the Flash (SWF) and SVG (Scaleable Vector Graphic) formats.

Flash is a proprietary format, even though it is so widely available. SVG, however, is in its infancy. It has been conceived as an open format, and as part of the latest HTML specification. Like Flash it has animation and user interaction capabilities.

The world of bitmaps has moved on too; other formats like JPEG and PNG display all 16.7 million colours, not just the 256 available to the GIF. Like GIF they are compressed, but unlike GIF the degree of compression can be more effectively controlled.

Size

Although computer monitor proportions are 4:3, browsers can display full screen or be dragged to a smaller window size, and they can also be configured with customised toolbars. Monitors themselves also vary in size, and the bigger they are, the higher the resolution (dpi) they display. So the size of the computer 'canvas' is unpredictable. These are important considerations when creating Web animations. Remember also that the unit of measurement for Web animation is not millimetres or inches, but the pixel.

5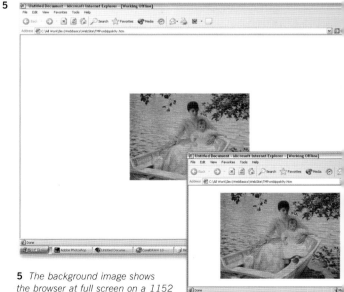

5 *The background image shows the browser at full screen on a 1152 x 864 pixel resolution monitor, while the inset image is at 640 x 480 pixels. Look at the result!*

16   CREATING AN IMAGE

Here we've created some sample images for use in Web animation, so you can look at all the options available in vector and bitmap formats.

Vector option (left–hand page)

A new 400 x 300 pixel document has been set up here in a vector drawing application, CorelDraw. Text has been added, the word 'FLOAT' set in Futura Bold, 24 point and centred. (Points are the default unit for type, but once your image is defined in pixels, it doesn't matter what measurement system you use within it.) The text is filled with a red that has the RGB value 215/32/50.

We don't need to edit the text, but want to move and rotate the individual letters. To do this, the text needs to be converted to curves or outlines. Next we've drawn a rectangle-like shape with a wavy top and filled it with a blue of RGB value 0/172/246. The transparency of the blue is set to 80 per cent of the solid value, so that the red text shows through. Then we've returned to the original blue fill and edited the wavy line to make it choppy. The letters here have been rotated and rearranged so that they are bobbing up and down, and the transparency reapplied to the blue. Finally, the parts of the letters below the waves have been distorted. An alternative to a flat blue fill is a *Linear Blend* from blue at the bottom to white at the top, using Corel's interactive transparency feature.

In summary, a vector application has fantastic text handling ability, and can easily be used to edit and distort both drawings and text. It also has crisp edges and, of course, scalability without distortion.

Bitmap option (right–hand page)

For this we've used Photoshop. Once again the text has been created and the blue shape added. Using Photoshop's *Wave Distortion* filter, the shape can be amended. Wavelength, amplitude and scale can each be edited to create the desired choppiness. Before the text can be distorted, though, it needs to be rasterized, which means it loses its properties as text and becomes an image to which further effects

A typical vector application like CorelDraw can create all the effects shown here. They are scalable without loss of quality, but realism is lacking.

1 *Vector strengths include good text handling.*

2 *Easy-to-draw linework.*

3 *Vector transparency.*

4 *Easy-to-manipulate letters and linework.*

5 *Easily distorted text outlines.*

6 *Transparent blends.*

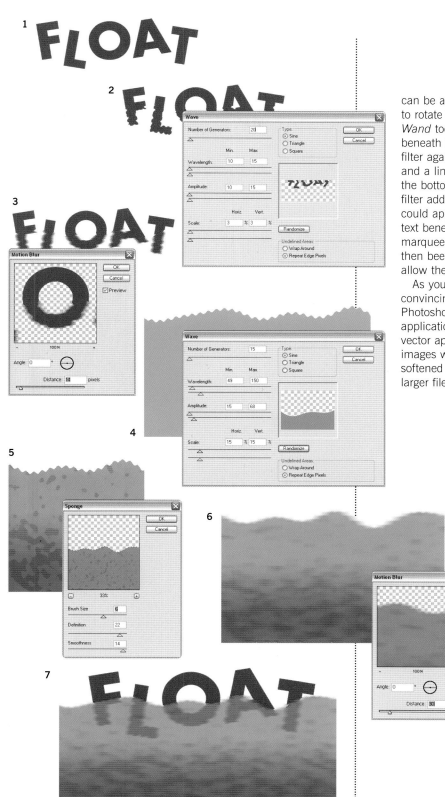

can be applied. We've used the *Free Transform* tool to rotate individual letters, followed by the *Magic Wand* tool to 'marquee select' the area of the text beneath the blue, and applied the *Wave Distortion* filter again. Next the blue layer has been selected, and a linear blend applied to make a darker blue at the bottom (R24/G86/B163). The *Artistic Sponge* filter adds mottling. To soften the mottling area, you could apply a *Motion Blur* to this layer. Finally, the text beneath the blue has been selected and the marquee expanded by 12 pixels. *Motion Blur* has then been applied to this layer. The extra 12 pixels allow the blur to extend beyond the letter shapes.

As you can see, the bitmap version is far more convincing, and this is merely a simple example. Photoshop – in common with all bitmap applications – offers greater artistic freedom than a vector application, particularly in its ability to blend images with partial transparency and create softened edges. But the disadvantages include larger file sizes and a lack of scalability.

A typical bitmap application like Photoshop creates multiple effects at the click of a mouse, but they are not scalable.

1 *Rotated text.*

2 Wave *filter applied to a masked area.*

3 Blur *filters are available.*

4 Wave *filter with extra choppiness.*

5 *You can add mottling using the* Sponge *filter.*

6 Motion blur *sponged image.*

7 *Combine the text and waves and the bitmap image is more realistic than its vector cousin.*

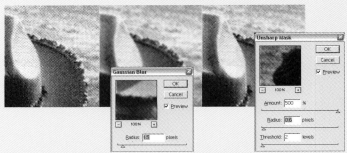

2

18 Scanning

A scanned image is always a bitmap image. If you scan an A4-sized landscape image at 300 dots per inch (dpi), it will be 3508 pixels wide, but the average monitor can only display just over 1000 pixels of width, and even the largest seldom measures more than 1600 pixels. Therefore, to capture as much detail as possible at this resolution, you need to reduce the image to less than 15 per cent of its scanned size to fit within an animation of 400 x 300 pixels. Therefore, don't scan any image until you have decided on the size at which it will be used.

The conversion from 'real world' sizes to pixels can be confusing in itself. To complicate matters further, a PC screen's resolution is slightly finer than a Mac's, as you can see from the table below. A bitmap image will appear onscreen at its actual (real-world) size only when it is a 96 dpi image on a PC, or 72 dpi on a Mac.

If you scanned a printed image from a magazine or newspaper (as opposed to a photographic print), the image will have contained a screen (the printing process uses a screen of coloured dots). Your scanner cannot correctly read the fine dots of a printed image, creating a 'moiré' pattern on the scanned version. Some scanners have a *Descreen* button to correct this problem. If yours doesn't, you can get a similar degree of correction using a bitmap application like Photoshop or Paintshop Pro. Apply a small amount of *Gaussian Blur* to soften the image, and then an *Unsharp Mask* to resharpen it slightly. Screened images should be scanned at higher resolutions, 300 dpi plus. For most other images, scanning at 150 dpi will suffice.

3

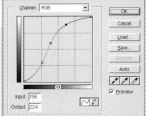

1 *Image widths in pixels at various dpi and their real-world mm equivalents*

2 *A coarse-screened image can be improved in a bitmap application like Photoshop by first applying a blur and then a sharpening filter.*

3 *Even on a modest flatbed scanner, you can scan objects like these. Leave the lid open, but place a sheet of white paper over the background if you want it to stay a light tone. The Photoshop* Curves *panel quickly improves the image.*

1

	72 dpi	96 dpi	150 dpi	300 dpi	600 dpi
	Mac screen	PC screen			
300 pixels	105.8mm	79.4mm	50.8mm	25.4mm	12.7mm
400 pixels	141.1mm	105.8mm	67.7mm	33.9mm	16.9mm
500 pixels	176.4 mm	132.3mm	84.7mm	42.3mm	21.2mm
3,508 pixels				297mm	
38 pixels		10mm			
28 pixels	10mm				

4 *If you don't scan with a piece of paper over the object, the background goes black, which can be useful at times. This piece of crumpled white paper has been masked, the background cut away and a Photoshop drop-shadow layer effect applied.*

5 *A specialist application like CorelTrace offers a range of accuracy and stylistic options when tracing a bitmap. This example uses an accuracy level of 60 using an outline trace.*

6 *In CorelDraw the results of the trace show how the image now comprises discrete vector shapes that can be edited and recolored.*

Image sources and resources

There are some picture resources where copyright might be an issue, such as magazines; books; newspapers; brochures and leaflets; banknotes; packaging; greeting cards; passports; badges; and stickers. It *may* be possible to use some of these items (not banknotes, however!), but approach with caution. You can, of course, experiment privately with such material, but not necessarily publish it on the Internet or burn it onto CD

On the other hand, there are plenty of image sources where copyright does not apply, such as your own artwork; very old publications (where copyright has elapsed); archives of royalty-free images; your family photographs; cutout shapes, like home-made decorations; flat objects like leaves, cogs or jewellery, and handprints or footprints.

Although scanned images are bitmaps, it is possible to convert them into vector images using a Trace application; CorelTrace was used to create examples 5 and 6 opposite. Of course, not all images are suitable for tracing: you need a clearly defined image with contrasting tones and colours. Trace software will try to find edges, then fill each area within them with a flat colour that matches the original. The result is similar to the *Posterize* effect in a bitmap application like Photoshop.

The outcome is a series vector shape that can be edited in a vector application, such as CorelDraw, Xara or Illustrator, and then saved in Flash or SVG format. Most Trace applications have settings to control the complexity of the resulting shapes, along with applied special effects like *Sketch* or *Woodcut*. As the examples show, tracing can be the source of some great visual effects.

If scanning hard copies isn't of interest – you might have some form of digital camera, for example, or want to work only with images that have already been digitized – you'll find that the Web is a great source of copyright-free material. There are plenty of sites offering free clip art or photographs. In fact, you might find that you have a clip art library bundled with your graphics software.

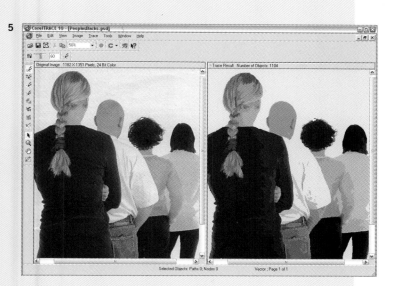

20 STARTING TO ANIMATE

Before starting to animate, let's look more closely at the software applications you will need. These include a GIF assembler application like Adobe ImageReady, Macromedia Fireworks, GIF Builder or GIF Construction Set. Next you will need a Web design DHTML application like Macromedia Dreamweaver, Adobe GoLive or FrontPage; a Flash animation application like Macromedia Flash, CorelRave, Swish or LiveMotion; a vector (graphics) application like CorelDraw, Adobe Illustrator, Macromedia Freehand or Xara. Finally, you'll need a bitmap (paint) application like Adobe Photoshop, Photopaint or Paintshop Pro.

Of course, there are numerous alternative applications, including shareware and freeware ones, and many vendors allow you to download a 'save disabled' or time-limited version of their leading products for you to try out.

Because we've already looked at the differences between vectors and bitmaps, we will concentrate here on the assembly of the actual animation itself.

GIF Animation

Adobe ImageReady was used to create the animated GIF projects in this book. ImageReady uses Photoshop's native PSD file format, adding extra animation instructions to any Photoshop file. For example, open a Photoshop file with three layers (see the myMusicMan.gif example opposite). In the ImageReady *Animation* window, you will see the first frame of a new animation that includes all the layers which were visible when the file was opened. Click *New Frame* and a second identical frame will appear. Alter the content of the second frame by turning the visibility on or off for each layer. Click *New Frame* again and repeat the process until you have created all the frames you require for your animation. This is a very effective way to create a GIF animation but, if you prefer, ImageReady will simply assemble an animation from imported, or pasted, flattened files.

❶

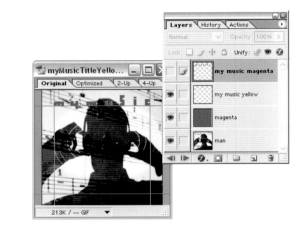

❶ In ImageReady, create the layers and then select which layer you want to be visible in each frame. Set the time delay for each frame if you don't require an even frame rate (see Timing text, right).

❷

❸

❹

❺

❻

Tweening

If you select two adjacent frames, ImageReady will automatically create intermediate frames between them (hence 'tween'). Tweening softens the animation but requires little or no frame delay to create this smoothness. Although this can be a useful timesaver, adding frames of course adds to the file size.

Timing

The speed at which a GIF animation plays is controlled by the addition of a pause (delay) between frames. An animation may require a constant frame rate of, say, 0.2 seconds' delay for smooth delivery; another may require a jerky action or perhaps a long (four-second) pause – for a headline to be read, for example. By selecting *all* the frames in your animation, you can control the frame delay globally.

A GIF animation will always play every frame, so a very large file on a slow Internet connection will simply slow down and your timings will be compromised. So ensure that your animation is as lean as possible; it is often feasible to break a larger image down into several smaller animations.

❷ Select two frames from an animation and then choose *Tween*.

❸ If the default *All Layers* is selected along with *Add 5 Frames*, ImageReady will use all visible layers to create these extra frames.

❹ Frame 2 has now become frame 7; five new in-between frames have been created.

❺ Smooth tweens can also be created between objects of different sizes.

❻ Here 10 extra frames have been added by *Tweening*. The resultant animation shows a pulsing circle.

22 Optimization

ImageReady, in common with most GIF assemblers, has a number of tools that will optimize your animation for the Web. Most important is the *Colors Reducer*. Reducing the number of colours will significantly decrease the file size. For example, the five-frame 200 x 200 pixel animation shown opposite is reduced to eight colours, resulting in a file size of 15kb, but if you increase it to the maximum of 256 colours it becomes an unsustainable 95kb.

If your proposed animation includes many subtle, varying colours, it will be difficult to reduce them to a limited palette without ruining your creation, so GIF may not be your best medium. Remember that if you reduce the colours to eight, for example, then that number will apply to every frame in the animation, not just the first.

The next tool is lossy compression. This reduces file sizes by selectively discarding data. You can use the slider to see how much loss is acceptable. Dithering can also be applied. When the colours are severely reduced, dithering can help by simulating colours that are not available. This is best applied on a trial-and-error basis using the slider. There are three suboptions: diffusion (usually best), pattern and noise.

The other options are of little benefit to GIF animations. For example, you should avoid using transparency or interlacing.

You may have heard the term 'Web-safe' (or 'Websafe'). This was most relevant when people's monitors displayed only 256 colours, which is not the case with more recent models. A problem arose because the 256 colours available to a Mac were not all the same as those available to a Windows PC. There were, however, 216 that were common to both, and these became known as Web-safe. At the time, the *Web Snap* tool offered a variable, rather than absolute, match of these colours. So the Mac OS, Windows and *Web Snap* options can also be ignored here.

One final thing to remember: when you have completed the optimization process, don't forget to use the *Save Optimized As* option, or all your hard work will come to nothing.

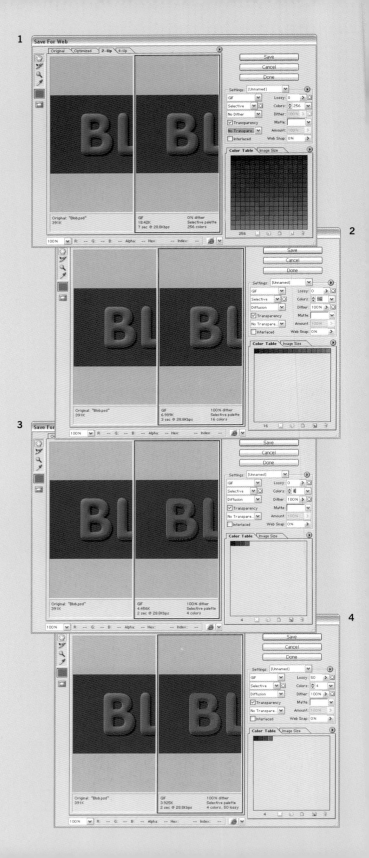

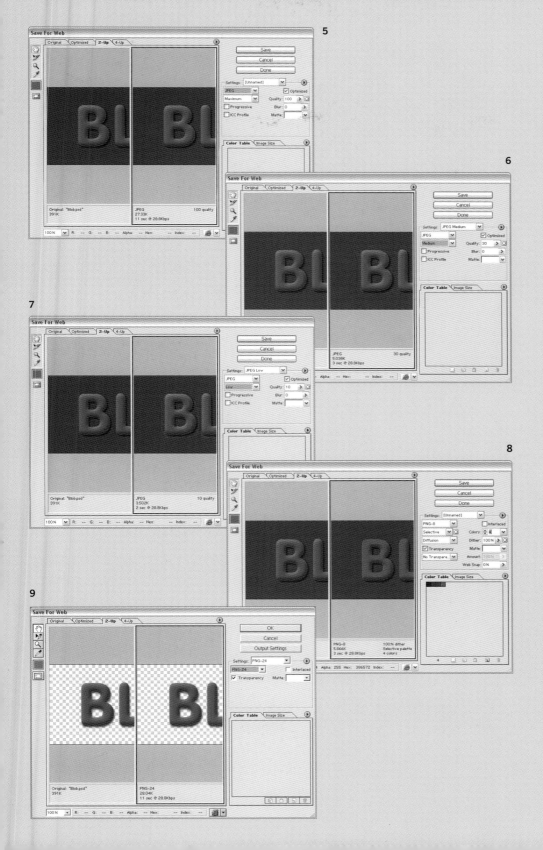

When you *Save for Web in Photoshop*, this is the panel you will select from. Let's look at the GIF option first.

1 Here, GIF Colors are set to maximum 256, No Dither. File size: 18.65kb.

2 GIF Colors at 16, Diffusion Dither. File size: 6.61kb.

3 GIF Colors at 4, Diffusion Dither. File size: 4.29kb.

4 GIF Colors at 4, Diffusion Dither, Lossy 50. File size: 3.66kb.

Now let's look at JPEG.

5 JPEG Maximum quality 100. File size: 27.10kb.

6 JPEG Medium quality 30. File size: 5.00kb.

7 JPEG Low quality 10. File size: 3.47kb.

Finally, let's compare PNG formats: PNG-8 is the GIF equivalent (the 256-colour version looks identical to the GIF and is not shown).

8 PNG-8 Colors at 4, Diffusion dither. File size: 5.61kb.

9 PNG-24 Colors cannot be specified, so the file size is excessive. In common with the GIF, a transparent background can be specified (JPEG does not allow for transparency). File size: 28kb.

24 DHTML Animation

Creating animations in DHTML is quite different to doing so with GIFs. While a GIF is constrained within a shape and has virtually no means of interactive control, a DHTML animation is constrained only by the browser window and can be driven by a wide range of JavaScript controls. (Don't worry. You won't have to bother learning JavaScript, because these controls are built in to most Web design applications).

Before you consider using DHTML as your animation medium, it is important to recognize one key factor: DHTML operates by placing every item in a 'container' that is, confusingly, called a layer. But as you will see, its functions are rather different to the layers in Photoshop. When you create a layer in DHTML, using a program such as Dreamweaver, a rectangle appears, the coordinates of which are automatically recorded like a map reference. (This is measured from the top left-hand corner of the browser window to the top left-hand corner of the layer.) If the browser window is only 800 pixels wide and the layer is at a position 900 pixels left, it will not be visible without scrolling, which would render any animation unworkable. So the animation has to be tailored to fit a browser window – it cannot be dynamically recentred in the browser the way an image within a table can be.

Once you have decided on the size of browser window in which your animation will be displayed, you can set to work. Dreamweaver is the application used to create all the DHTML animations in this book.

You now know that DHTML animations use layers, but how can these be moved around? That is the *Timeline*'s job. This is a chart that logs changes to a layer (or layers). To enable the recording of any change in a layer's position, a new keyframe has to be added to the timeline. Keep adding a keyframe and dragging your layer to a new position, and you will have created a DHTML animation. It's that simple. Obviously the layer has to be filled with something; as a simple exercise you can just fill it with a colour, as we do in the DHTML primer on page 34.

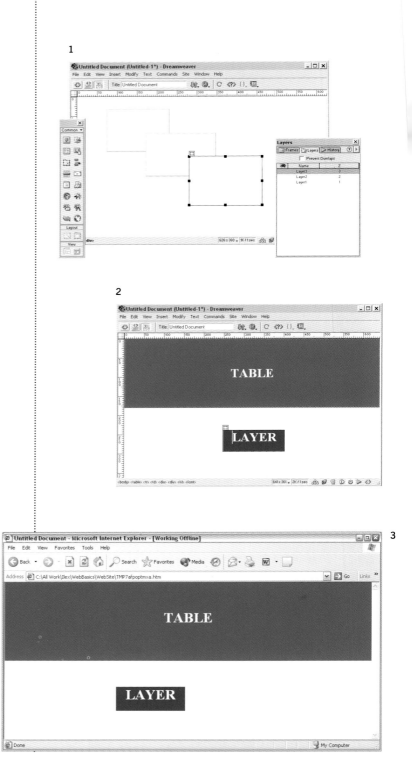

1

2

3

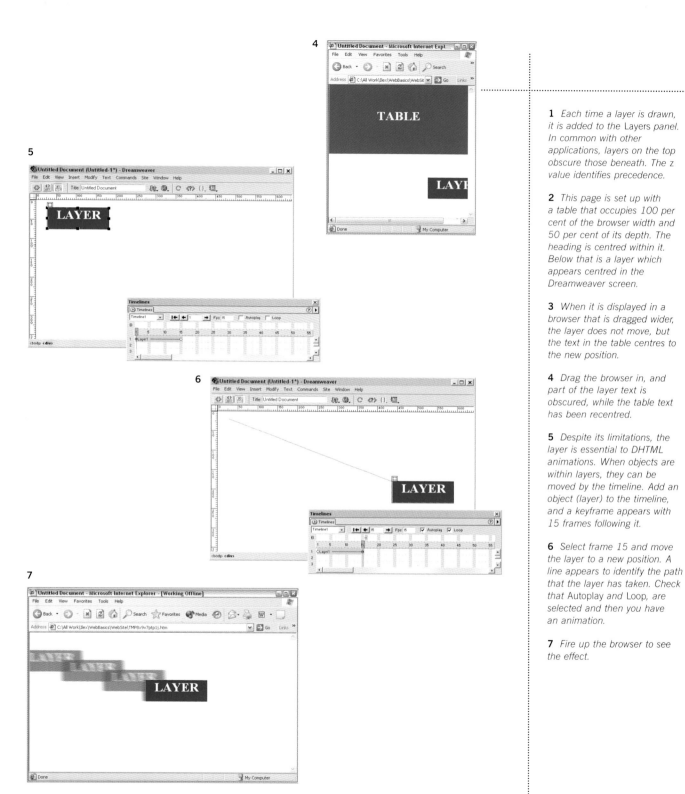

1 *Each time a layer is drawn, it is added to the* Layers *panel. In common with other applications, layers on the top obscure those beneath. The* z *value identifies precedence.*

2 *This page is set up with a table that occupies 100 per cent of the browser width and 50 per cent of its depth. The heading is centred within it. Below that is a layer which appears centred in the Dreamweaver screen.*

3 *When it is displayed in a browser that is dragged wider, the layer does not move, but the text in the table centres to the new position.*

4 *Drag the browser in, and part of the layer text is obscured, while the table text has been recentred.*

5 *Despite its limitations, the layer is essential to DHTML animations. When objects are within layers, they can be moved by the timeline. Add an object (layer) to the timeline, and a keyframe appears with 15 frames following it.*

6 *Select frame 15 and move the layer to a new position. A line appears to identify the path that the layer has taken. Check that* Autoplay *and* Loop, *are selected and then you have an animation.*

7 *Fire up the browser to see the effect.*

Adding images

You can place any image in a layer as long as it is saved in one of the recognized Web formats: GIF, JPG/JPEG, PNG, SWF and finally (although not all applications currently allow it), Scalable Vector Graphic (SVG). This is a new format promoted by some software makers but ignored by others.

There are two ways of moving a layer after having first selected it. You can either open the *Timeline* window and select *Add Object* to add one keyframe, followed by another one 15 frames later. Select the second keyframe and move the layer to the desired new position and a bar will be added between the two keyframes. Continue adding keyframes within this bar and move the layer each time. Drag the keyframes up and down the timeline to control the pace of the animation.

Alternatively, after selecting the layer, you can choose *Modify > Timeline > **Record Path of Layer*** and drag the layer on any course around the page. A trail will be left behind it, and when you release the mouse button, the trail will stop and you'll see that keyframes have automatically been inserted on the timeline. Whichever method you choose, you will notice that it is the top left-hand corner of the layer that is attached to the path.

As you can see, layers are at the heart of DHTML animation. Although layers are visible by default, it is possible to make them invisible. On page 120 a visible layer with a right-facing fish 'swims' towards the right, but when it reaches its destination it is made invisible and replaced by a left-facing fish within another layer. This becomes visible and swims towards the left of the tank. The processes involved are explained in more detail within the project itself.

The timeline can autoplay when the page loads and loop continuously, or you can set it so that buttons and other devices control it. At the top of the timeline is a separate B channel that is used for adding in 'behaviours', such as inserting a sound at a particular point. The most common control is a start and stop behaviour, applied not to objects within the timeline itself, but to an object outside the animation, such as a control button. DHTML animation is, therefore, not like GIF animation, but is a great preparation for animating in Flash.

Flash Animation

To recap: a GIF animation is a single file that resides within a normal HTML page; DHTML animation is the dynamic control of layers in an HTML page; while Flash is a total environment for creating animation.

Like DHTML, Flash uses a timeline and keyframes to assemble and control animation. But while the DHTML timeline has separate channels in which to animate each individual layer, the Flash timeline uses layers instead of channels, which can be confusing if you use both environments. However, the big advantage that Flash offers animators is that objects on its layers can have varying degrees of (Alpha) transparency, so that layers beneath the top one can show through. A keyframe is created automatically at frame 1 when you start placing content on a new layer, but you can also create a blank keyframe first and begin drawing in it.

When completed, a Flash animation is exported as a Flash movie. Even the most complex Flash movie with hundreds of images, thousands of words, and complex interactive user features is still a single SWF file. Outside the Web environment, it can be played independently from a browser, but inside it a Flash movie needs to be placed within a single HTML page for it to function. This is what happens when the entire site is Flash. More commonly, though, Flash is used within an otherwise conventional HTML site to liven it up.

Flash has another tremendous virtue in that it is vector-based, which results in small, scalable files. But Flash can also happily mix bitmap images with vector ones, and even apply vector effects to bitmap images. In many ways, it is the animator's and designer's dream come true.

So what are the downsides? Well there are very few in Flash itself – some Flash intros take a long time to download, but this is really the fault of the designer/animator who will have made them too complex. The *Shape Tweening* function doesn't work very well, but is intended to morph two versions of the same image. Also, the interface and some of the tool functions can be idiosyncratic, and very old browsers may not include the Flash plug-in. But really these are minor quibbles.

The Flash screen has a lot of panels. This brief tour shows the one that you will be using in the projects.

The main Flash window comprises the timeline and the work area (stage) below. The animation is assembled by adding keyframes to the timeline and by adding the objects to be animated to additional layers.

The lower part of the Tools panel displays different information depending on which tool is selected.

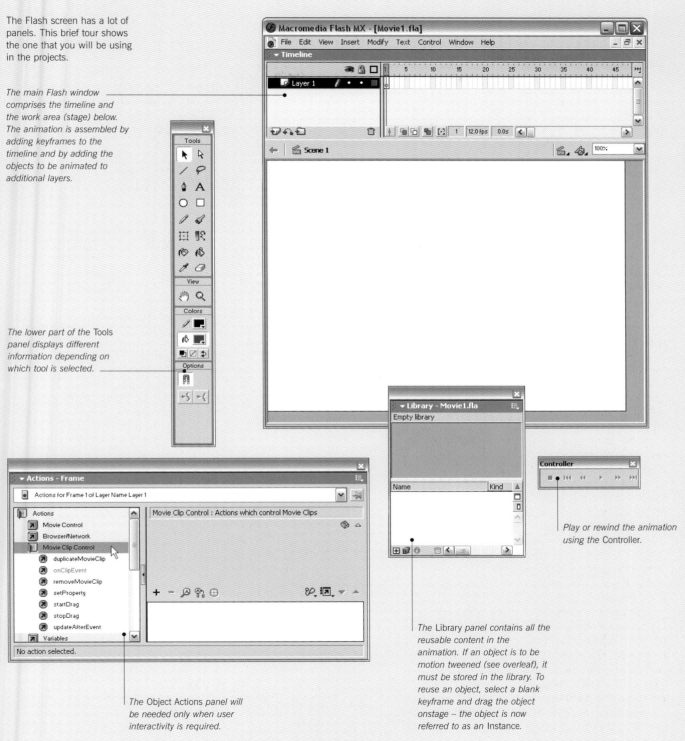

Play or rewind the animation using the Controller.

The Object Actions *panel will be needed only when user interactivity is required.*

The Library *panel contains all the reusable content in the animation. If an object is to be motion tweened (see overleaf), it must be stored in the library. To reuse an object, select a blank keyframe and drag the object onstage – the object is now referred to as an* Instance.

Ready? Set? Go!

So how do you get started with Flash? First define the movie's dimensions using *Modify > Dimensions* and keep the *Ruler Units* as pixels (this area is called the *Stage* in Flash). The basic structure of the timeline has been described, so the next most important feature is the *Library*. The *Library* is a store for all the objects included in your animation, whether images or text. Flash calls them *Symbols*. A symbol can be repeated within an animation, but it remains just one object, which helps keep the final file size from escalating. Each time a symbol is reused it is called an *Instance*.

An instance can be changed without the original in the library being altered. It can be transformed – rotated, stretched, squashed, skewed and scaled. Its colour and (Alpha) transparency can also be altered. Drag an *Instance* onto the *Stage*, in a new layer, and a keyframe will automatically be created. Using symbols produces another benefit, particularly with text: if you need to change a symbol, then all instances that occur throughout the animation will automatically be changed as well.

Hitting the Symbols

There are three types of symbol: a *Graphic*, a *Button* and a *MovieClip*. Regular objects and text are normally graphics. Buttons are self-explanatory – Flash provides built-in actions for a button, and a pointing finger appears over it to show that it is active. A Flash movie can also be converted to a *MovieClip* symbol, that can be reused just like any other symbol.

Next on the feature trail is *Tweening*. First, *Motion Tweening*, which is the ability to generate the in-between frames that occur between two instances of a symbol in separate keyframes. This is a truly labour-saving feature that allows very rapid development of your animation ideas. *Motion Tweening* can also be used to fix an object to a path. *Shape Tweening* is the other tweening method; it is akin to *Morphing*, but is less useful because it is restricted to simple objects. Even then it is quite difficult to use.

There is a wide range of user controls that can be included in a Flash animation. These are similar to

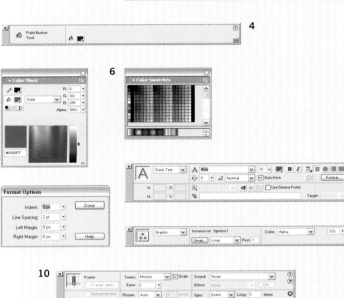

These are the most used panels...

1 Info *displays the size and location of an object.*

2 Transform *is for rescaling and simple distortions – these can be better performed using the* Modify *dropdown menu.*

3 Stroke *is the outline that is added when the* Rectangle *or* Circle *tools are used. Remember to set this to Nil on the* Tools *panel before drawing if you don't want an outline.*

4 *Use* Fill *to select a colour. For gradients, select each colour using the* Color *selector on the* Mixer *panel.*

5 *Within the* Mixer *panel you can select the Alpha value to control the transparency of the colour.*

6 Swatches *are not very useful. It is best to use the* Mixer *to access the full range of colours.*

7 Character *enables font size and tracking to be controlled using sliders.*

8 *Apply simple paragraph formatting using the* Paragraph *panel.*

9 *The* Effect *panel also controls the Alpha transparency and other colour functions to symbol instances.*

10 *Probably the most important item of the entire Flash interface,* Effects *enables you to add* Motion Tweening *between two Instances on the timeline, and Shape Tweening between two objects on the timeline that are not* Instances.

11 *This is a typical Flash screen. Another layer has been added, an example object has been saved as a symbol and a second keyframe has been added. Motion tweening has been applied and a new feature,* Onion Skinning, *turned on so that the progress of the animation can be seen.*

12 *Using the* View *dropdown menu, you can view the stage cropped to the animation size or see a wider work area.*

the JavaScript Behaviors in Dreamweaver, but in Flash they are called *Actions*, and *ActionScript* is the code that drives them. Once again, *ActionScript* will be generated automatically, but if you are a programmer it is possible to extend actions by writing your own scripts. As in DHTML, these actions can be added to keyframes in the timeline, or to buttons. If a Flash animation gets too big and unmanageable, it is possible to break it up into Scenes. These normally play consecutively but, if required, actions can also trigger them to play in any order you require.

Flash has a reasonable array of vector-drawing tools, but customized vector applications like Illustrator, Freehand, CorelDraw and Xara are better for sophisticated drawing. Images created in them can then be imported into Flash. In addition to this, Flash has some specific bitmap editing tools, but again it is best to import bitmap images from your favourite application.

As objects in Flash animations often move 'off-stage' (outside your film's actual dimensions), you will need to have *View* > **Work Area** selected so that you can manipulate them. Deselect this option to see the animation cropped to actual size.

What next?

We have now looked at the three main 2D Web animation technologies, and it is time for you to try them yourself. The following projects have been devised to introduce all the previous concepts in a real animation setting. The first time that you see a GIF, DHTML and Flash animation will be within a very simple primer project that will get you up and running – and eager to try the more complex projects that appear later in the chapter!

11
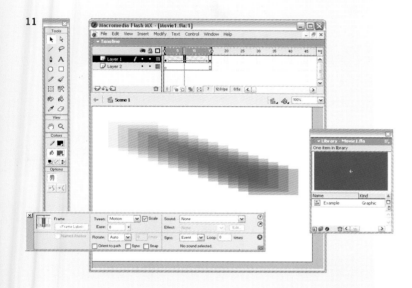

12
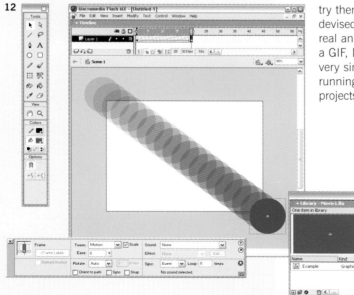

PART 2

The Projects

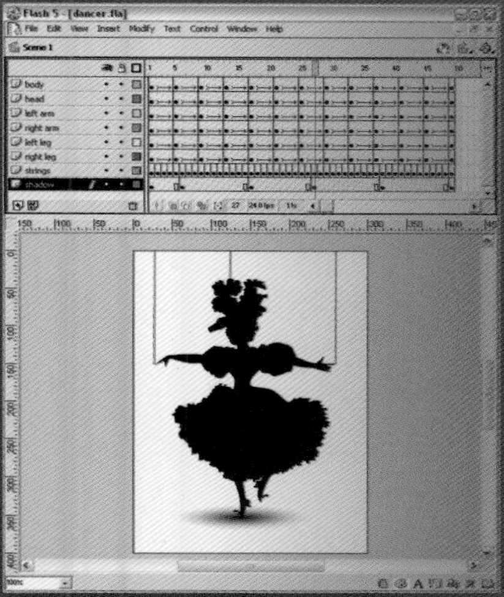

Web Expert: Animation **is not limited to the pages of this book. Still images can never represent an animation adequately, so a dedicated website,** ***www.webexpertseries.com/animation*** **has been set up. All the animation projects in this chapter can be viewed on the site and you can download them and see how each one works. You can even replace the images with your own and, with most Flash animations, you can change the text by simply editing the text symbol stored in the library.**

32 *WEB EXPERT*: ONLINE

All the ancillary files used to create the animations have also been included on our website at *www.webanimation.web-linked.com*. To open these, you will need a copy of the application that created each one. If you don't have a particular application – Photoshop for example – you can usually successfully import the files into a similar one, like Photopaint or Fireworks. The files on the site are in PC format, but they can also be opened on a Mac (the major applications are all cross-platform these days). The website also has an extensive links section, which will direct you to many of the online resources available, as well as showcasing sites where you can see the very best in Web animation. Who knows? Our own animations may soon be among them!

The most effective way of learning Web animation is by creating your own. This book and the accompanying website provide you with a kit that you can spend time experimenting with.

A word about the fonts

For copyright reasons the fonts used in the following projects cannot be provided so, where necessary, you will have to replace them with those available on your own system. In addition to the main font suppliers, there is a huge variety of free fonts available on the Web. Be warned, however, that they are usually the 'oddball' ones, often poorly designed, but there are occasional gems among them, so it is worth searching through. The fonts used in Flash animations (SWF files) are embedded so they will display correctly. However, the editable Flash source file (FLA) that was used to create each animation will not include the font.

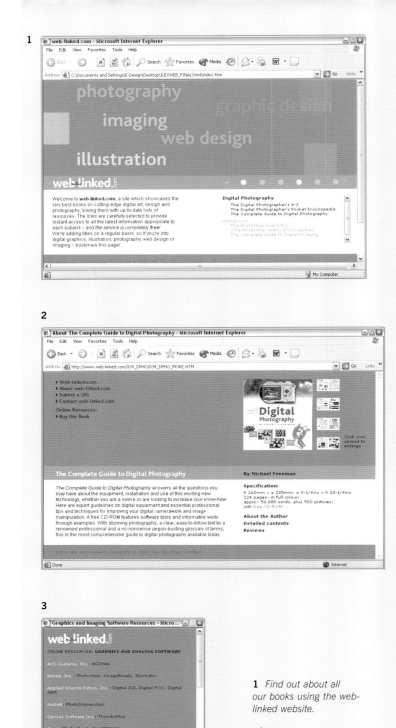

1 *Find out about all our books using the web-linked website.*

2|3 *Each book that you purchase has a link to an invaluable, dedicated Resources area that is regularly updated.*

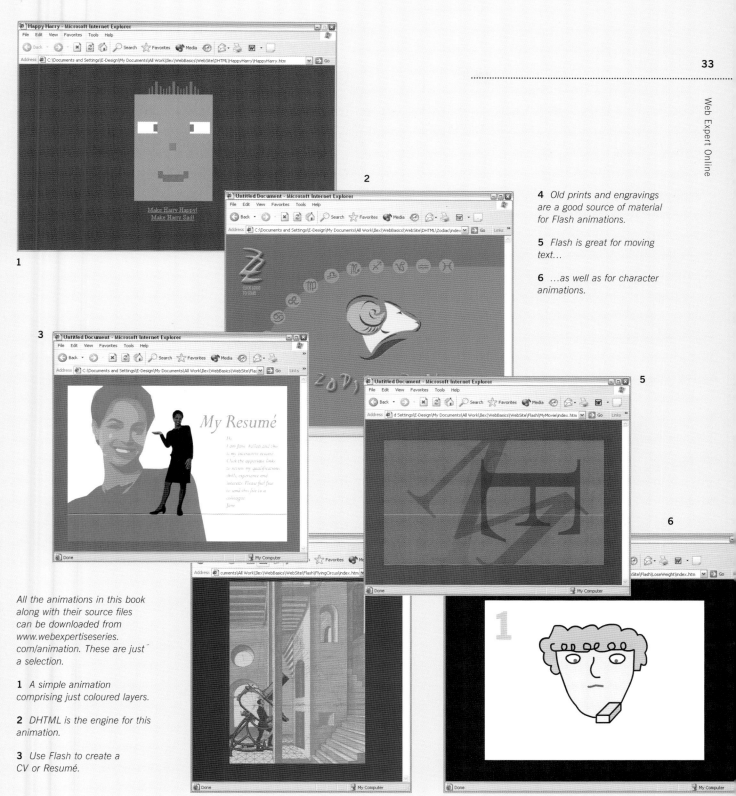

4 Old prints and engravings are a good source of material for Flash animations.

5 Flash is great for moving text…

6 …as well as for character animations.

All the animations in this book along with their source files can be downloaded from www.webexpertiseseries.com/animation. These are just a selection.

1 A simple animation comprising just coloured layers.

2 DHTML is the engine for this animation.

3 Use Flash to create a CV or Resumé.

34 HAPPY HARRY

As this is our first project, we've kept it really simple. There are no imported images: Harry is made from coloured rectangles that are either visible, or not. They are turned on and off by moving a mouse over the captions. There is no animation software involved either: we've used Web design package Dreamweaver.

The result is a standard webpage (HTML file). But this means there is one problem to overcome: there are no tools for 'drawing' in a Web design application, since the current HTML specification would not recognize them. So, instead of drawing rectangles you will have to create layers.

In this context, layers are simply placeholders or containers normally used to position text or images, but they can also be filled with colour. The position of each layer is fixed by a coordinate, x pixels from the left and x pixels from the top. The image is made using 14 layers filled with appropriate colours; most of these stay visible all the time, only those forming the mouth and the eyes change.

When you wish to duplicate a layer, use the *Copy* and *Paste* commands. The new layer can also be dragged to a new location if necessary. Remember that layers on the top will obscure those beneath.

Why his hair has text appeal...

Rather than adding another 15 layers to create each of the strands of spiky hair, we've used text. A single layer contains a sequence of lower-case 'L's formatted as Arial/Helvetica, sizes 5, 6, 7, 6, 5, etc. It looks like this...

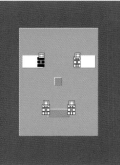

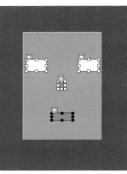

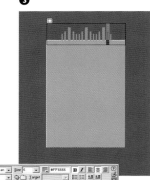

7

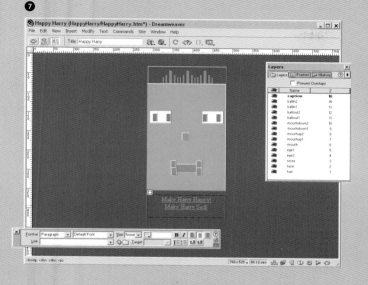

8

9

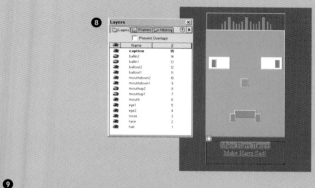

1 Create a new document using your favourite Web design application. For this, we used Dreamweaver. The window size is 768 x 525 pixels. Select *Modify > Background* to define the colour and the text links.

2 Go to *Objects > Layers* to draw a shape, 196 x 276 pixels in size, and fill it with the lilac background (Bg) colour. In the *Layers* panel, name this shape 'Face'.

3 Add a new layer below and call it 'Hair'. Using a sans serif font put in a repeated sequence of lower-case 'L's at sizes 5, 6, 7, 6, 5 to simulate spiky hair, using pink as the text colour.

4 All the remaining layers will be added above the Face layer, so add four more features using the *Layer* tool and name them Nose, Eye 1, Eye 2 and Mouth, applying colour using *Properties > Bg Colour*.

5 Add a further four layers, naming the eyeballs Ballout1 and 2, and the shapes to form the 'sad', downturned mouth as Mouthdown1 and 2.

6 Add a further four layers naming the eyeballs Ballin1 and 2, and the shapes to form the 'happy' upturned mouth as Mouthup1 and 2.

It is the two sets of images created in steps 5 and 6 that will be animated.

7 Add one final layer named Caption, and type the two lines of text that will control the animation. (This screenshot shows all the layers as visible.)

8 Hide the two 'Ballin' and two 'Mouthup' layers by clicking on each layer until the closed eye icon appears. Highlight the text 'Make Harry Happy!' and in *Properties > Link* add in a '#'. This enables a Javascript behaviour to occur without an actual link to another page. Repeat the process with the text 'Make Harry Happy!'

9 Open the *Behaviors* panel and, with the text still selected, click the '+' sign and select *Show-Hide Layers*. Make *OnMouseOver* the event that triggers the behaviour.

10 From the panel you can now also select the layers that will be shown or hidden. When the mouse is over the 'Make Harry Happy!' text, Mouthup should be shown and Mouthdown hidden, Ballin shown and Ballout hidden.

11 Highlight the text 'Make Harry Sad!' and apply the process again, this time reversing the layers that are hidden and shown. Test the animation out in your browser.

10

11

36 EYE CONTACT

This project is your first GIF animation. We've discussed the theory, and now you are going to put it into practice! Remember that most GIF animation applications are fairly basic because they simply assemble a sequence of images and control the amount of time that each is displayed for.

Although the images were created here in Photoshop/ImageReady, any bitmap editor and GIF assembler could be used. The eye images are created using the *Ellipse* tool, and the eyeballs are on separate layers to the eye whites so they can be moved independently of each other. The animation comprises eight frames with a two-second delay between each. Frames seven and eight are repeated a further three times, this time with a zero-second delay. (The zero delay makes the eyes blink rapidly.) Duplicating frames saves effort, but doesn't reduce the GIF file size. The image is black-and-white, so reducing the original 256 colours to eight will decrease the file size successfully. The black and the white account for two colours, while the other six (greys) are required for antialising.

Hiding under an antialias...

If the GIF has not been antialiased, the curved parts of the images would appear stepped, but the file size would be even smaller because it would comprise just two colours, black and white. If it is enlarged it will stay sharp-edged, even though the steps will of course get bigger.

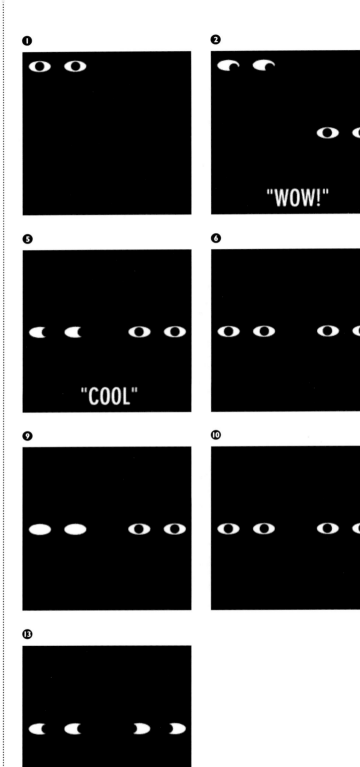

❸

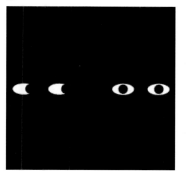

❹

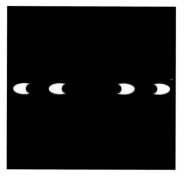

❼

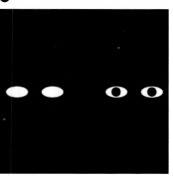

❽

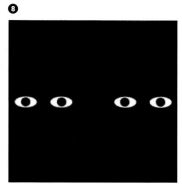

⓫

⓬

Create a new Photoshop/ImageReady document, sized 200 x 200 pixels. Fill layer 1 with black.

Using the *Elliptical Marquee* tool, define the white area of the eye on a new layer and fill it with white.

Using the same tool, define the eyeball and fill this with black.

Using the *Text* tool, create the words 'COOL' and 'WOW' per illustration on separate layers.

❶ to ⓭ Having created the raw material, move the image on each layer to form one frame of the animation. Use *Copy Merge* to create all 13 frames of the finished animation, as shown in the sequence, *left*.

⓮ The ImageReady animation panel shows the frame delays; initially set at two seconds, then reduced to zero seconds for the blinking eyes, and finally a pause of six seconds before the animation restarts.

⓮

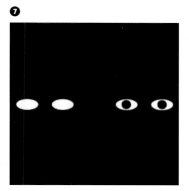

38 SNOWBOARDER

Now you can start experimenting with moving an image across the browser window. As with the Happy Harry project, we've used DHTML (within Dreamweaver), but now the timeline is deployed to control the number of steps (frames) that the snowboarder takes to get from point A to point B.

First, though, the images have to be created. The snowboarder is actually a piece of vector clip art that has been exported as an antialiased GIF, optimized to eight colours. The snowy cliff is a simple vector drawing, also exported as a GIF, but optimized to just two colours. It is not necessary to antialias the image because the pale blue and the white background are similar in tone.

Although the animation extends across the 800-pixel browser window, the snow cliff needs to be larger in case the animation is viewed on a higher resolution monitor. By using it as a background image, the snow cliff will automatically tile (repeat) to any browser width. So to avoid a repetition of the cliff being visible, the white background is increased so that it covers a 1200 x 1000 pixel area. It is a two-colour image, so the file size is a tiny 4kb, despite the extent of the image. The snowboarder takes 15 frames to travel the distance, at a frame rate of 15 frames per second (fps).

When GIFs go off piste

If you save the snowboarder in SVG format, it can be enlarged without any loss of quality. However, if you want to enlarge the GIF, you will have to go back to the vector source file, enlarge it and then re-export it as a new GIF.

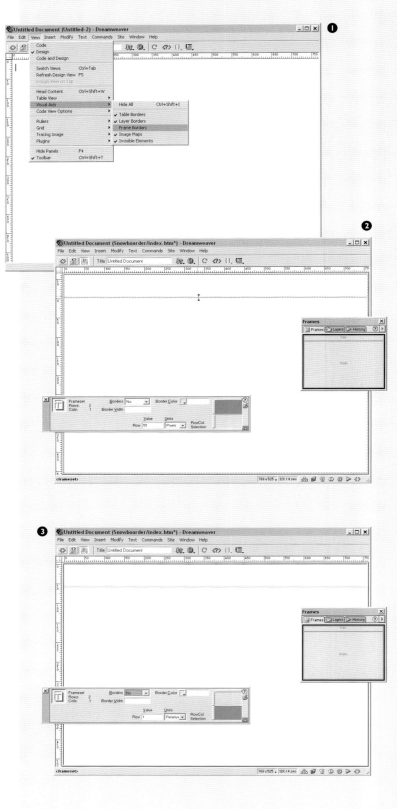

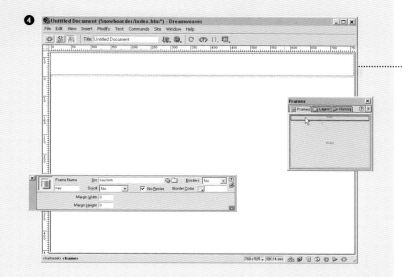

❶ Open a new document using your favourite Web design application. Dreamweaver was used here, with a window size of 768 x 525 pixels. Select *View > Visual Aids > Frame Borders*. This will allow you to see the extent of the frameset in which the two webpages will sit. (These borders will not be visible in the browser.)

❷ From the top of the document window, drag a frame down to 55 pixels and set *Borders* to *No*.

❸ Within Properties, click on the lower frame miniview to select it. Then select *Row > Relative* and set this to a value of 1. This will have created an invisible frameset in which two HTML pages will appear. The upper frame will be of a fixed depth, while the bottom one can be dragged to any size.

❹ To complete the frameset, click on *Frames > Mini View > Top Frame*. In the *Properties* panel name this 'Nav', then click on the lower frame to name it 'Main'. Ensure *Scroll* and *Borders* are set to *No*, that *No Resize* is selected, and the *Margins* are set to 0.

❺ Place the cursor within the Nav frame and go to *File > Save Frame*. Name this 'nav.htm' before repeating the process with the lower frame (naming this one 'main.htm').

❻ Click on the horizontal grey line that is the boundary between the two frames, and select *File > Save Frameset* to name it 'index.htm'. You should always name a frameset this way if is to be your homepage, but if a frameset appears elsewhere in your site you can name it anything you like.

40

7 Go to *Object* > *Layers* to draw a layer shape within the nav frame large enough to contain the title image. Place the cursor within the layer and use *Insert Image* to select a suitable file. The one shown here is named 'title.gif'.

8 Place the cursor within the main frame and go to *Modify* > *Page Properties* > *Browse* to select a background image. For this example, we selected background.gif, which is 1200 x 1000 pixels. This is far larger than the target browser size of 800 x 600, so the image will automatically position itself in the top left of the frame. This means the excess image will only be visible to someone with a monitor set to a high resolution if they drag the browser out to full screen.

9 Go to *Object* > *Layers* and draw a shape 170 x 170 pixels. As before, place the cursor within the layer and use Insert Image to select a suitable file. The one here is named 'snowboarder.gif'.

10 The timeline will be used to move the snowboarder from top left to bottom right. Initially drag the layer to a position under the title. Keep the *Timeline* panel visible and go to *Modify* > *Timeline* > *Add Object* to Timeline. The snowboarder will then appear as a 15-frame section of the timeline.

11 Click on frame 15 of the snowboarder's timeline and drag the layer to the finish position at the bottom right. A line will appear to join the start and finish positions.

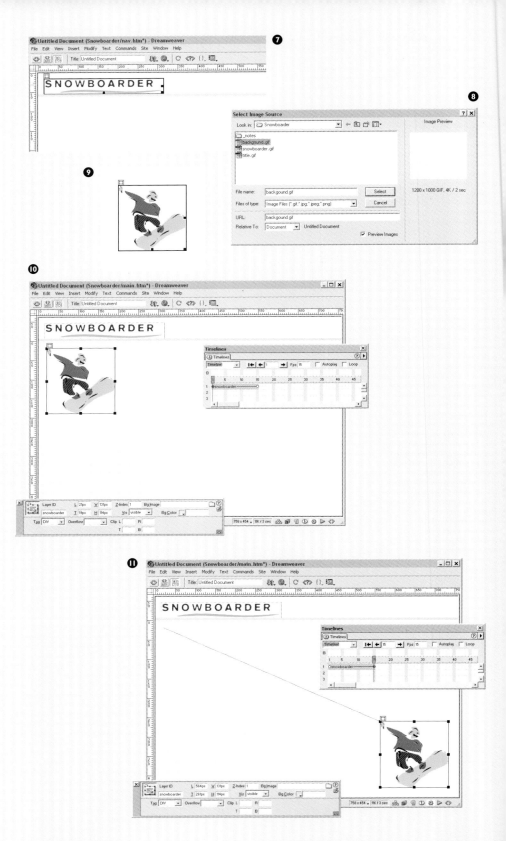

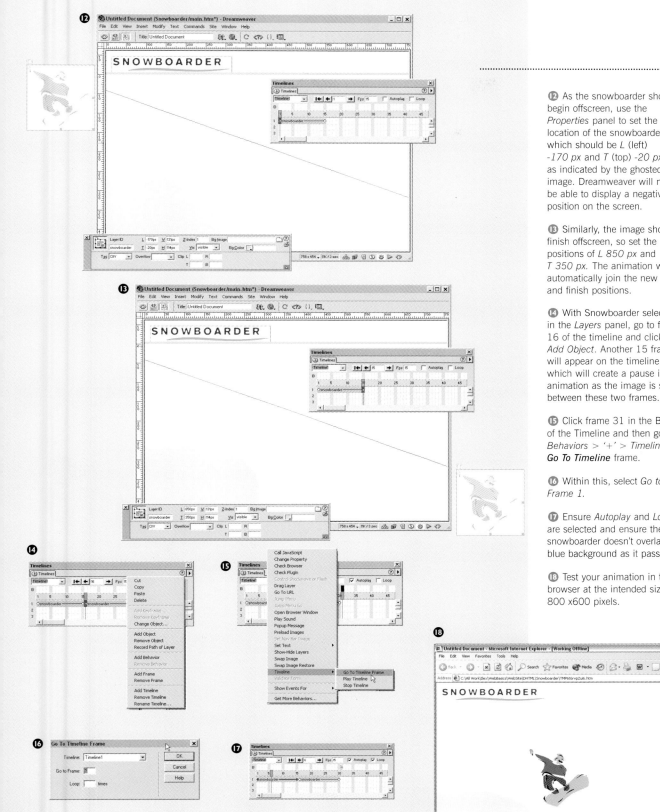

⑫ As the snowboarder should begin offscreen, use the *Properties* panel to set the location of the snowboarder, which should be *L* (left) *-170 px* and *T* (top) *-20 px*, as indicated by the ghosted image. Dreamweaver will not be able to display a negative position on the screen.

⑬ Similarly, the image should finish offscreen, so set the positions of *L 850 px* and *T 350 px*. The animation will automatically join the new start and finish positions.

⑭ With Snowboarder selected in the *Layers* panel, go to frame 16 of the timeline and click *Add Object*. Another 15 frames will appear on the timeline, which will create a pause in the animation as the image is static between these two frames.

⑮ Click frame 31 in the B row of the Timeline and then go to *Behaviors > '+' > Timeline > Go To Timeline frame*.

⑯ Within this, select *Go to Frame 1*.

⑰ Ensure *Autoplay* and *Loop* are selected and ensure the snowboarder doesn't overlap the blue background as it passes.

⑱ Test your animation in the browser at the intended size of 800 x600 pixels.

42 DUCK PARADE

In this project you will make a simple duck image waddle across a rectangle. A black-and-white clip art (vector) image was used in this example. This is made from a collection of grouped parts; after ungrouping them, you can apply colour to each area and the two legs can be separated from the body. The legs can easily be distorted so that one stretches forwards, the other back. The image is exported in EPS format, which allows it to be opened (and rasterized) in a bitmap application without it having a white background.

You could draw your own duck and scan it. If you do, remember to draw the legs detached from the body. The white background will then have to be removed and the image put onto a new layer. Once converted into the bitmap domain (using Photoshop or ImageReady), the image can be reduced to the desired size, then split up and pasted as new layers.

If your bitmap application is unable to display each frame with its own layers don't despair: you can copy merge all the layers, required for each frame and paste them individually into a blank document, from which you can then assemble your animation. Alternatively, if you're using a very basic GIF assembler, it may be necessary to save each frame as a separate file. This will probably need to be a JPEG, but check the application to see the recommended options.

When you are ready to assemble the animation use an application like ImageReady, which has an animation window in which you can manage individual frames, and a layers window.

Duck souped up

If you use an application like Photoshop or ImageReady, then give your animation a professional look by applying a 3D layer effect to each duck image. To further enhance the animation, apply a graduated background to give an appearance of depth.

❶ Here is our original duck.

❷ You now need to prepare your duck. In the example shown here, the clip art image is deconstructed using CorelDraw, and the legs are separated from the body using the *Node Edit* tool. (Other applications refer to 'anchor points' rather than nodes.)

❸ Apply colour to each area.

❹ Now export the duck in EPS format so that its background is transparent. Open in Photoshop at 72 dpi – the chequerboard shown here indicates transparency.

❺ Create a new Photoshop document, sized 285 x 180 pixels. Use the *Rectangular Marquee* tool to define the blue area and fill this with colour – try RGB 158/191/235.

❻ Reduce the size of your imported duck so that it fits the new document, and copy the body and each leg separately, pasting them all into different layers – one set over the body (Leg A) and the other (Leg B) beneath it.

❼ Now give each layer a name, such as 'Body', 'Leg A Behind', and 'Leg A Forward'. The leg that is furthest away, Leg A Forward, should be a lighter tone than the other, so go to the *Layer* slider to reduce the Opacity to 60 per cent.

❽ Copy each of the three layers and name the new layers 'Body Copy', 'Leg B Behind', and 'Leg B Forward'. This time reduce the layer opacity of Leg B behind to 60 per cent. Your two ducks should now look like this.

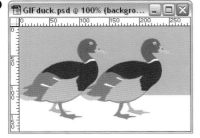

9 Now *Copy Merge* the layers Body, Leg A Behind and Leg A Forwards and paste them all as a new Layer 1. Move this to the extreme left of the frame.

10 Repeat the process using the layers Body Copy, Leg B Behind and Leg B Forward, and move the resulting new Layer 2 left but just ahead of the previous layer.

11 Continue pasting layers using the alternate Body/Leg combination until the frame is filled (which should take ten layers).

12 Turn off the visibility of all layers except Layer 1 and the Background. The next stage is to switch to ImageReady to assemble the animation.

13 Select Layer 2 and turn off Layer 1. Use the Arrow button to add a new frame, and leave all options unselected.

14 Continue selecting layers and adding frames until you reach the end, ensuring that the Background layer is visible on all frames.

15 Adjust the frame delay so there is a three-second pause on the last frame.

16 Finally, use the *Optimize* panel to define the parameters for your animated GIF. Reduce the colours to just 12 with *No Dither* and use *Save Optimized* to complete the process.

17 This shows the completed ten frames.

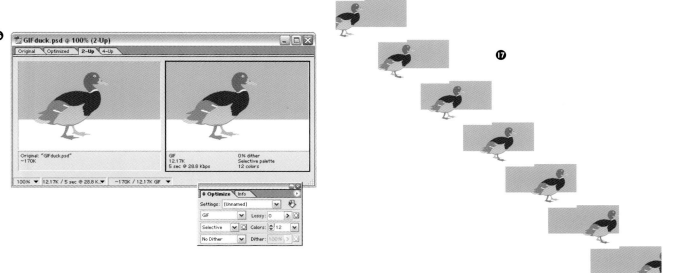

46 MY FAMILY AND ME

For this project you will return to DHTML and learn
how to control multiple objects on the timeline. The
objects consist of individual layers, each containing
an image. The position of any layer in the browser
is fixed – it will always be x pixels from the top and
left regardless of whether you drag the browser
window larger or smaller.

The project includes a set of 'curtains' that open
from the centre of the window. To do this, you must
first fix the window size (see our tip below). The
'curtains' consist of a single GIF image, 400
x 520 pixels. Although the browser size is fixed at
800 x 600 pixels, the window within it can vary
between about 450 and 500 pixels in depth,
depending on how the menu bars have been
configured by the user.

The example animation illustrated here has been
designed for the default Windows IE Explorer
browser setting, and so has a depth of 469 pixels,
but only about 460 pixels are visible. If you want
to play safe you can make the curtains deeper, say
520 pixels. The image should be half the width of
the browser window, i.e. 400 pixels.

After the 'curtains' have opened, a series of five
photographs and subheadings are revealed and
then hidden in a sequence that has been set out on
the timeline. Spend some time getting familiar with
managing objects on the timeline. Try varying the
delays between objects appearing and disappearing.

Code up your browser size

Some Web design applications have built-in
methods of controlling things like the browser size in
which your animation displays. If yours doesn't, you
can paste in the following piece of HTML code.

```
<SCRIPT>
window.resizeTo(800,600);
</SCRIPT>
```

Ensure that code and put it between the <HEAD>
flags on your page. You want it up that high so that
the browser resizes before the rest of the page loads.

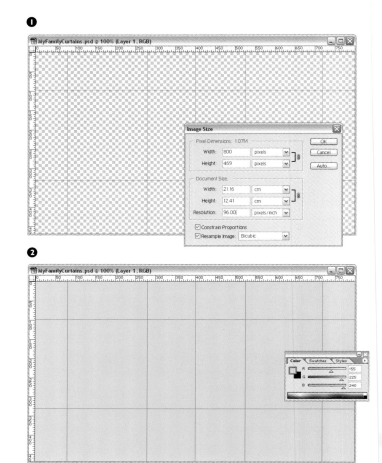

4

5

6

❶ It is convenient to prepare the animation in an application like Photoshop, since each image can be placed on a separate layer, allowing you to make adjustments to size or picture quality. Open a new document, 800 x 469 pixels in size, making it 96 pixels per inch if you are working on a PC and 72 dpi if you are working on a Mac. Add vertical guides at the centre and also at either side, 125 and 318 pixels away from the centre. Add horizontal guides at 100 and 332 pixels.

❷ Add a new layer and fill it with your preferred colour. We've used blue RGB 155/225/240 here.

❸ Create an image for the curtain that is half the width of the document. If you use a pattern, as here, ensure that the pattern will join properly with the one on the other curtain.

❹ Drag the curtain image out to the outer guideline. This will be the position of the open curtain.

❺ On a new layer beneath, create the curtain shadow. Using the *Marquee Select* tool, draw a shape to fit the area of the open curtain, but make it seven pixels wider. Use the *Gradient* tool set to *Black to Transparent*. Position the tool on the guideline and click and drag the cursor to the edge of the *Marquee* tool before releasing.

❻ The gradient will look like this when it is applied.

48

7 Copy and paste this layer. Go to *Edit > Transform* and rotate the image 180°, then position this new image at the left-hand side of the document. Select *Layers > Shadow Opacity* and change this to 30 per cent. This image will form the background to the final HTML page.

8 Go to *File > Save for Web > Optimize*. In this panel define the parameters; lock the background colour to blue by selecting it and clicking on the *Padlock* icon. Reduce the colours to six, select *No Dither*, and choose *Save Optimized*.

9 On new layers start adding the photos/images that you will use in the animation, scaling and cropping them to fit the guidelines.

10 Now start adding the text, also on new layers. To create the text as shown here, use the font Myriad Tilt in a colour that matches the blue/grey curtain background: RGB 77/112/120. Also go to *Layer Style > Drop Shadow* to apply a shadow. Use the default values, but reduce *Opacity* to 40 per cent.

11 When you have assembled all the images, select each one individually. Use *Copy* or *Copy Merge* to select an item, paste it into a new document (which can be discarded later), and from the *File* menu select *Save for Web*. Use the *Optimize* panel to define the parameters for your GIFs as before. For the titles, reduce colours to 16, for the curtain set them at four, but make sure all have *No Dither* selected and then use *Save Optimized* to complete

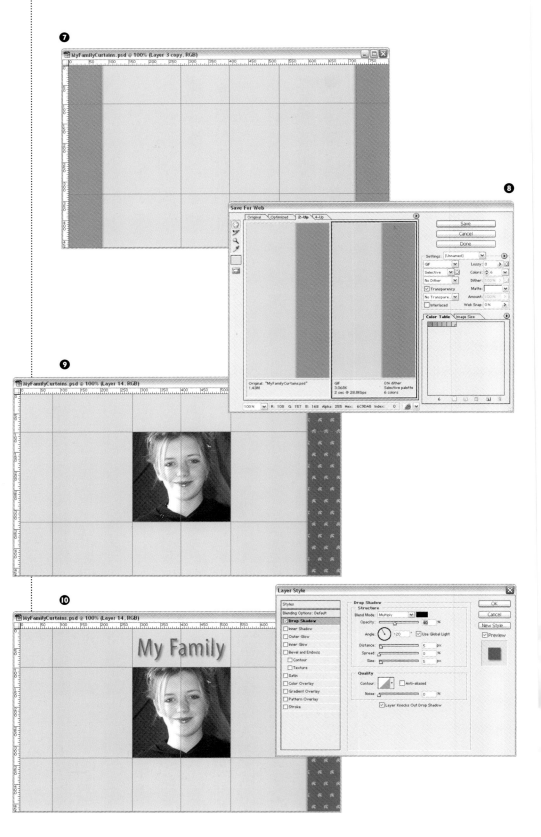

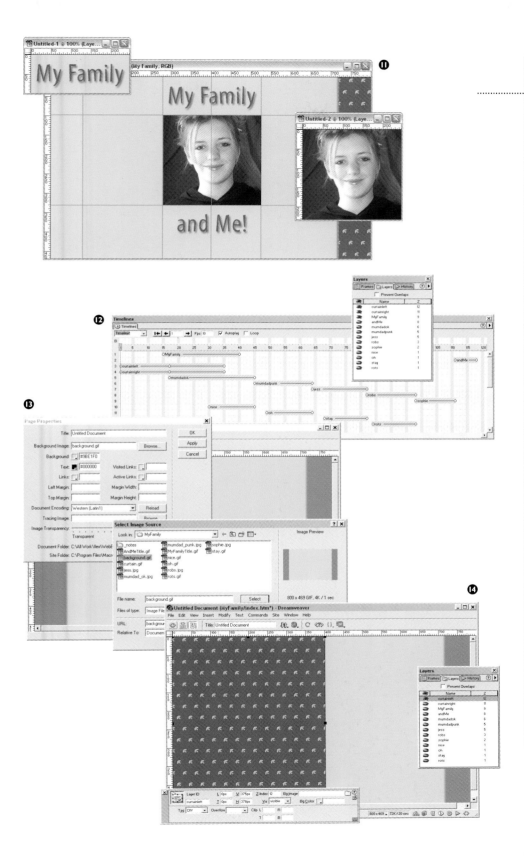

the process. The photographs should be saved in JPEG format. Use all the default values except for *Quality*. Use the slider until you are happy with the *Quality* setting – about 40 should be okay.

⑫ You now need to use a Web design application, such as Dreamweaver, to assemble the animation. Each element of the animation will appear in a separate Dreamweaver layer and as a separate entry on the timeline. Take a look at the two panels shown here to see the completed animation. Events on the timeline are staggered – there is a Curtainleft and a Curtainright, but both use the same image that you created earlier. The title 'My Family' emerges as the curtains part, and a succession of images and titles appear and disappear before the animation ends with the 'And Me' joining 'My Family'.

⑬ Go to *Modify > Page Properties > **Background Image*** and select the GIF that was created in step eight.

⑭ From the *Tools* panel draw a layer, place the cursor inside the layer and use *Insert Image* to select the curtains image. If the layer is too small, it will automatically enlarge to fit the image. Go to the *Properties* panel to position the layer to *L 0px and T 0px*. Repeat this process with the right curtain. (The *Layer Z* index can be ignored. As long as the layers are stacked in order of visibility, they will appear correctly.)

50

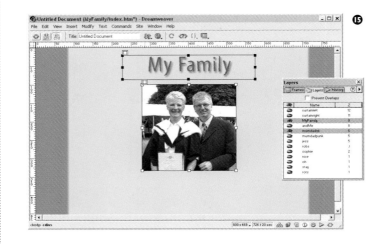

⑮ Add two more layers, 'MyFamily' and 'MumDadOk', and insert the appropriate images. The curtain layers have been hidden, otherwise they would obscure the new layers.

⑯ Now return to the timeline. Although the completed timeline has been shown in step 12, each element has to be added to it individually. Use *Modify > Add Object to Timeline* and select Curtainleft. It will then appear as a 15 frame section of the timeline.

⑰ Use the arrow and select *Add Keyframe* and then move the second and third keyframes to frames 17 and 35. At frame 35, drag the layer containing the curtain to the open position.

⑱ The animation will start with the curtain static between frames 1 and 17 and then it will open between frames 17 and 35. Repeat this process with the other curtain – at frame 23, they will look like this. The 'My Family' layer appears at frame 15 and persists through the entire animation to frame 118.

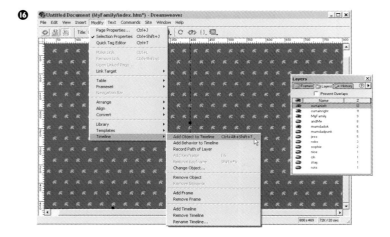

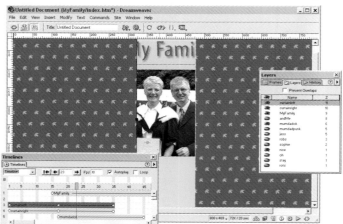

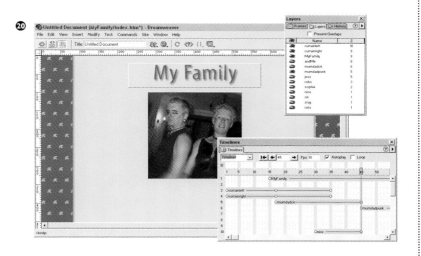

⓳ At frame 30, a layer we've named 'Nice' makes an appearance as the curtains open wider.

⓴ At frame 45 our layer 'MumDadOk' is now hidden and replaced by another, which we've named 'MumDadPunk'. The Nice layer is also now hidden. As you can see, the remainder of the animation is produced using the layers panel to show or hide layers at specific points in the timeline. Follow the screenshot shown at step 12 to accomplish this.

㉑ At frame 111 a final layer, 'AndMe', is revealed. This persists until frame 118, which is when the animation finishes.

㉒ Finally, to ensure that the curtain image loads first in the browser go to *Behaviors* > '+' > **Preload Images**. *Play Timeline* will appear automatically when *Autoplay* on the *Timeline* panel is select. You can also vary the frame rate until you are happy with the speed – 10 frames per second (fps) was used in this example.

52 STAR STRUCK

This is another DHTML animation, but this time you will design it so the browser can be maximized as the animated area is restricted to a region on the left of about 760 x 420 pixels. A large background image of 1600 x 1000 pixels is enough to fill even the highest resolution monitor without it repeating. We've kept it to a reasonable file size (8.66kb) by optimizing it to just six colours. This image contains a faded version of the 12 zodiac symbols. As the animation runs, 12 layers with 'full-strength' images positioned exactly above background symbols are made visible and then invisible in turn. These are synchronized with a further 12 layers that contain the zodiac illustrations. Each rectangular image contains a portion of background; this gives a better quality result than using the GIF Transparent Background feature (see our tip below).

As there are 12 pairs of objects, the timeline used to control the animation could become rather unwieldy. To avoid this, each pair of objects is visible for only five frames. This is done by reducing the frame rate down from the regular 15 to just four frames per second so each pair of images is visible for just over a second. Try varying the frame rate until you are happy with the result.

GIF backgrounder...

An antialiased transparent GIF will always include some pixels of the background colour from which it was made, so if the GIF moves across a different or variable colour background the smooth antialiased edge will degrade. You will obtain the best results if you use a constant background colour and create the GIF to match.

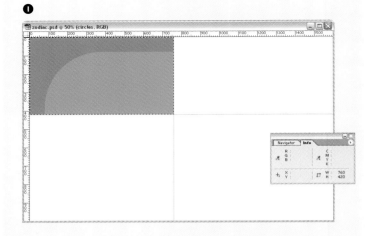

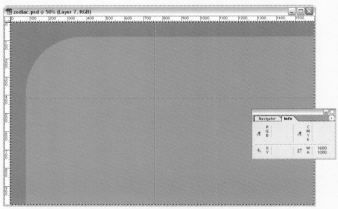

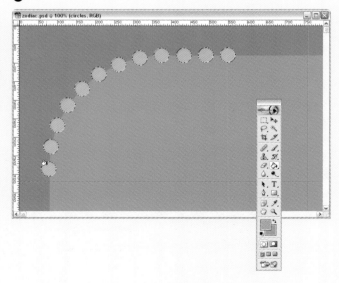

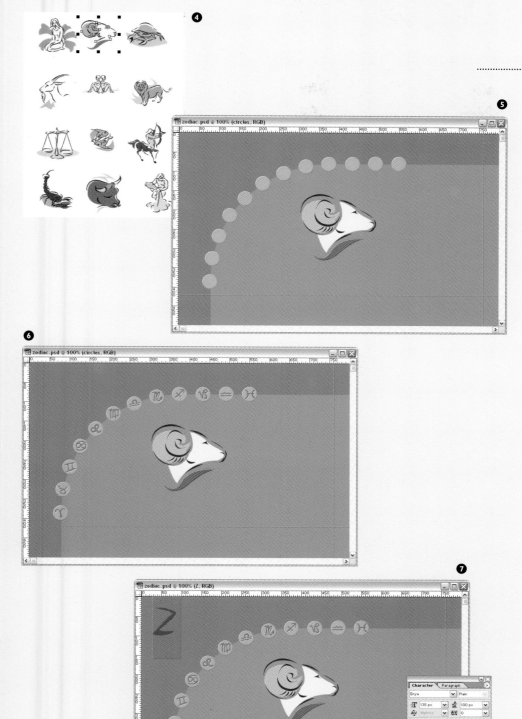

1 Create a new document, 1600 x 1000 pixels in size, using your favourite bitmap application (Photoshop was used for this example). Define an area 760 x 420 pixels at the top left. Go to **Tools > Marquee** to fill the area with a darker blue RGB 50/141/164 followed by a lighter blue-filled arc of RGB 75/161/182.

2 On a new layer beneath, continue the two colours so that they fill the entire area. This 1600 x 1000 pixel image will later be saved as the background image to the DHTML animation. In the meantime, concentrate on the area 760 x 420 pixels at the top left:

3 On a new layer draw 12 circles using the *Elliptical Marquee* tool and fill them with the orange RGB 241/169/92.

4 Either create your own or use imported clip art for the illustrations that represent the zodiac. If they are vector images (the ones shown here were created in CorelDraw), export them in EPS or AI format so that they retain a transparent background.

5 Open the imported illustrations and paste each into a new layer.

6 On a new layer above, paste the 12 signs of the zodiac. Again, either create your own or use imported clip art.

7 On a new layer create the ZZ device using a suitable font or draw it if you prefer. Enya was used here, at 135 point filled with the same orange used for the circles.

54

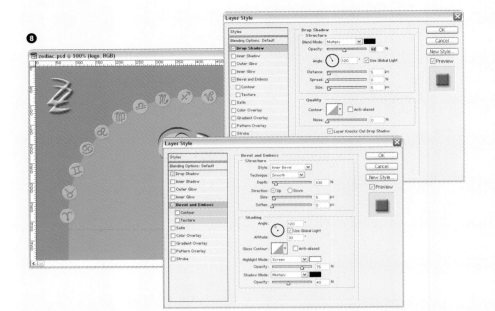

8 Go to *Layers > **Rasterize*** to convert the text into a graphic. Duplicate this image and overlap the second one on the first. If you have ended up with two layers, use *Merge Visible* to combine them, then go to *Layer Effects > **Shadow and Bevel*** to apply them.

9 On yet another new layer, create the main title in the manner just described, but adjust the size. Use *Rasterize* again, this time so the characters can be moved up and down. Finally apply the *Layer Effects*.

10 Select each area of the image in turn (*Tools > **Marquee Select***). Then *Copy Merge* and *Paste* each into a new document.

11 On the orange circles layer, reduce *Opacity* to 70 per cent. This will be saved as the background image for the HTML page (the 'full strength' circles will appear as the cursor passes over them).

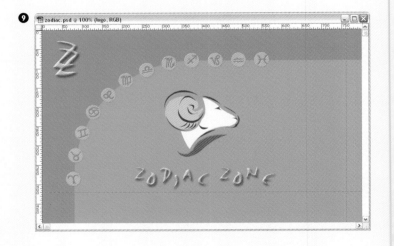

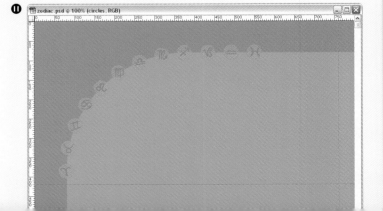

⑫Use *File > Save for Web* to select GIF as the format and optimize to eight colours. You should first select both shades of the blue background and lock them to make sure that they match the background image perfectly.

⑬ Continue with this process, selecting the minimum number of colours for each image, until all images have been saved.

⑭ Now assemble the animation (we've used Dreamweaver). Open a new document and use *Modify > Page Properties > Background Image* to select the GIF created in step 11.

⑮ Add a new layer for the title and the logo. Place the cursor inside the layer and go to *Tools > Insert Image* and select the images. If the layer is too small, it will automatically enlarge to fit the images in.

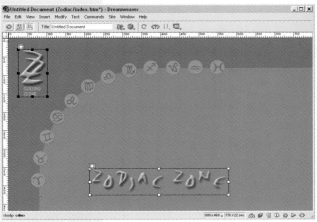

56

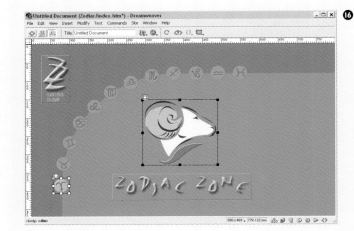

16 Add a layer for the first zodiac Illustration, Aries, and another for the small Aries circular symbol. Be careful to fit this exactly above the muted image on the background.

17 Continue this process until all the layers have their own images and are *in situ*. Layer names can't begin with a number, so use whatever naming strategy you prefer. Here an 'a' or an 'x' followed by a number has been used for identification.

18 With the layer x1 selected, go to *Modify > **Add Object to Timeline*** and x1 will appear as a 15–frame section of the timeline.

19 Continue this process with the layer a1 and then reduce both layers to 10 frames. Use the *Layers* panel to show and hide layers as required.

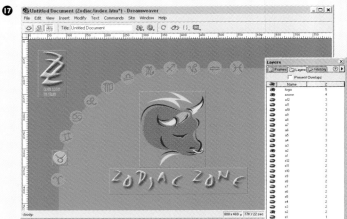

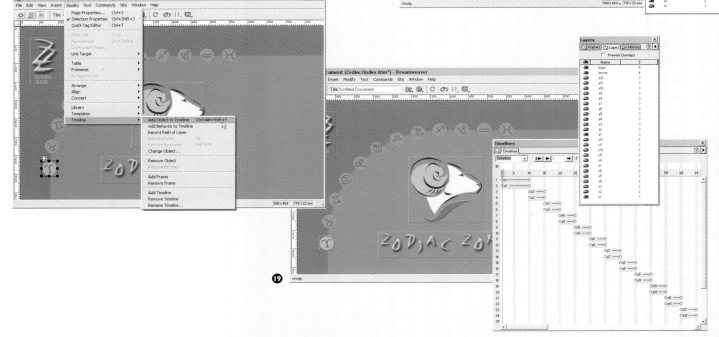

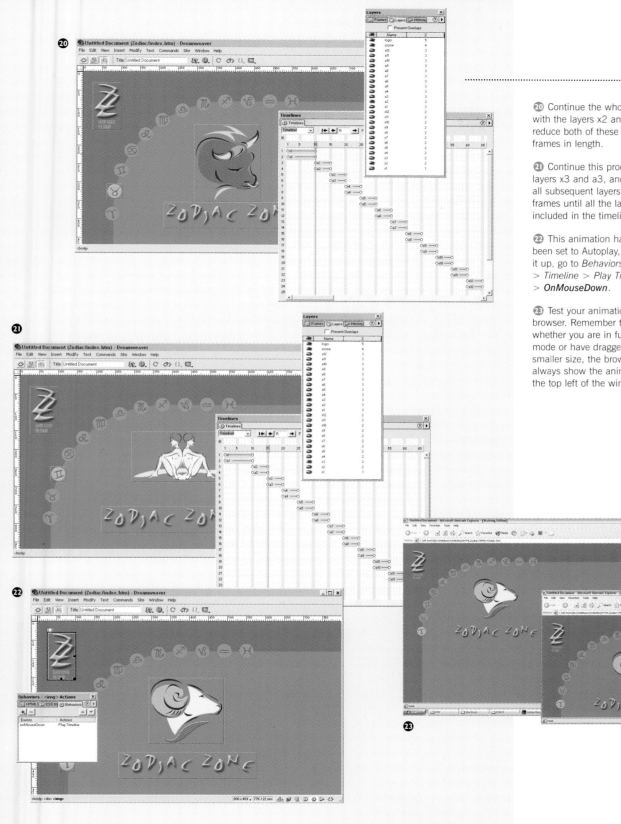

20 Continue the whole process with the layers x2 and a2, and reduce both of these to just five frames in length.

21 Continue this process with layers x3 and a3, and reduce all subsequent layers to five frames until all the layers are included in the timeline.

22 This animation has not been set to Autoplay, so to fire it up, go to *Behaviors > '+' > Timeline > Play Timeline > **OnMouseDown***.

23 Test your animation in your browser. Remember that, whether you are in full screen mode or have dragged it into a smaller size, the browser will always show the animation in the top left of the window.

58 THE BLOB

Morphing is a classic animation technique and it is surprisingly easy to do. In this project, the text is progressively deformed until it becomes a blob. The font used here is VAG Rounded Bold – you can quickly see why a rounded font will blend more convincingly into a blob than a sharp-edged one. Again, Photoshop and ImageReady are our applications of choice, because of their built-in 3D-style layer effects.

The master animation is 500 x 200 pixels in size and weighs in at a hefty 293kb. This is a convenient size to work with in ImageReady, but the final animation will be scaled down to 50 per cent and the colours reduced when we export it as an animated GIF. Until we can all enjoy high- bandwidth connections, animated GIFs are best kept to below 20kb.

It is surprising that this animation still looks good, even when the colour palette is reduced to just 32. You can see the trade-off between file size and quality on this book's website at *www.webanimation.web-linked.com.* There, 8-, 16-, 32-, 64- and 128-colour alternatives are shown along with relevant download times.

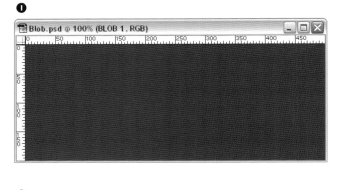

Any colour you like

To see how the animation would look in alternative colourways, use *Copy Merge* to create a new image, then use *Image > Adjust > **Hue and Saturation*** to vary the colours. If you find something you like, apply it to each layer before saving them in then animated GIF format.

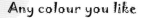

❸

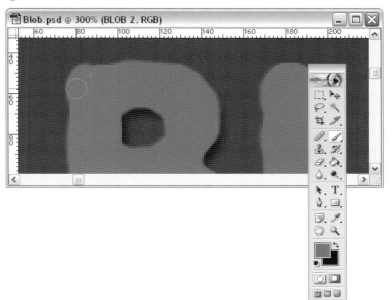

❶ Create a new Photoshop document, 500 x 200 pixels in size, and fill the Background layer with RGB 97/52/83.

❷ On a new layer create the word 'BLOB' using a suitably rounded font and fill this with RGB 0/130/130

❸ Duplicate the text layer and *Rasterize* it to make it into a graphic. Using the *Paintbrush* tool set to the text colour, deform the letterforms by spreading them outwards a little.

❹ Now duplicate this layer and continue the process until you have nine progressively deformed layers, the last of which should be a blob.

❹

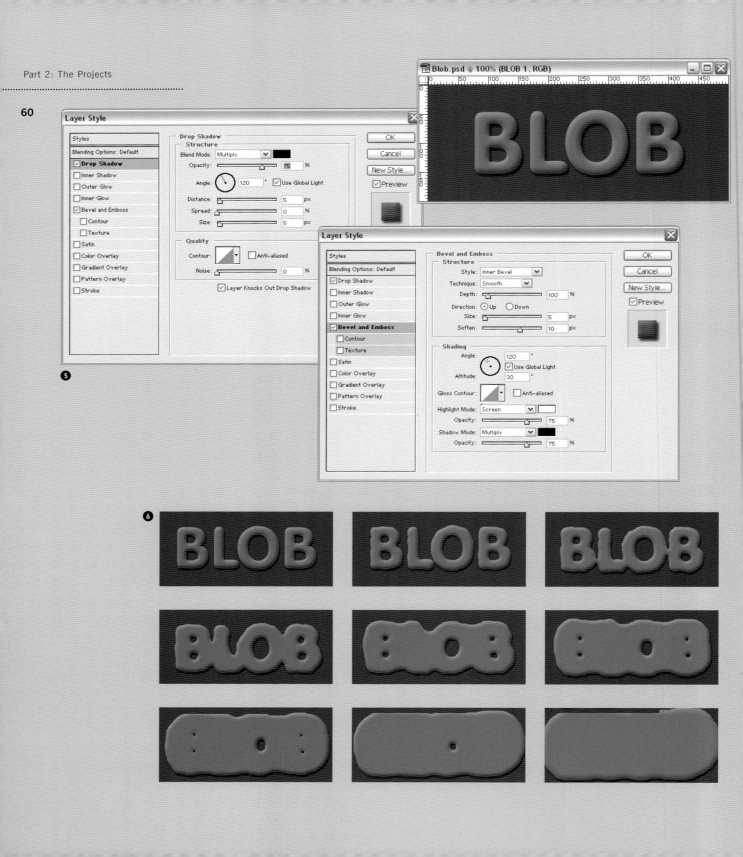

60

❼

❽

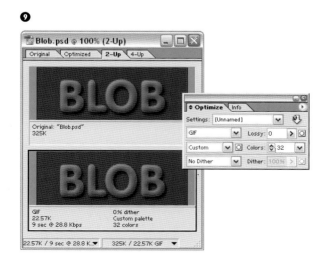

❾

❺ Return to Layer 1 and select *Layers* > **Add Layer Style**. Add a drop shadow and a smooth inner bevel from the *Bevel and Emboss* menu. If *Use Global Light* is left selected, any angle change to the drop shadow will automatically be applied in the *Bevel and Emboss*.

❻ Apply the layer style to each of the other layers by using the *Copy Layer Style* option and simply pasting it into each layer. The resulting images will look like this.

❼ From the *Image* menu, select *Size* and reduce this to 50 per cent.

❽ Turn off the visibility of all layers except Layer 1 and Background. The next stage is to switch to ImageReady to assemble the animation. Add frames by selecting the appropriate layer. A 0.5–second delay should be applied to all frames except the first, which should be two seconds.

❾ Finally, use the *Optimize* panel to define the parameters for your animated GIF. Reduce the colours to 32 with no dither, and use the *Save Optimized* option to complete the process.

62 MY MUSIC

Now you are going to try something really different.
You already know that it is possible to tile (repeat)
an image across a browser background, regardless
of the browser window's size. That background
image is normally a static one, but this project uses
a tiny (3kb) animation.

The way to create such a small file is to reduce
the number of colours the GIF contains. When a
bitmap image is created, it is usually antialiased
(see Glossary) by default. However, because the
font used here (Minimum) consists only of straight
lines, antialiasing can be turned off (within
Photoshop set antialiasing to *None*).

My Music includes a looped music file that plays
continuously until the viewer moves to another
page. The tempo of the animation should match
that of the music – in this case it is fast, but the
choice of music and, therefore, the tempo of the
animation, are up to you. You will also have to
build a homepage for the animation to appear in.
A six-frame frameset allows the browser to display
three pages simultaneously – the second contains
the heading images, while the first and third
contain the tiled background animated GI, etc.

The elements of the heading include the man's
head, the arrows (both are animated GIFs) and the
title itself, which is a static GIF. The frameset allows
some flexibility when you create the rest of the site.
For example you could keep frame 1 as it is,
change frame 2 into a navigation panel and use
frame 3 for the website content.

T I P

When jagged is good

As an alternative, try using a font with curves but
with antialias turned off – the normally unwanted
jagged edges can look interesting. The font will
have to be set very small (about 15 pixels) and
should be rasterized before being enlarged.
(Compare this to the other font, Stereophonic,
which is at 50 pixels in size set with antialias on.)

❶

❷

❸

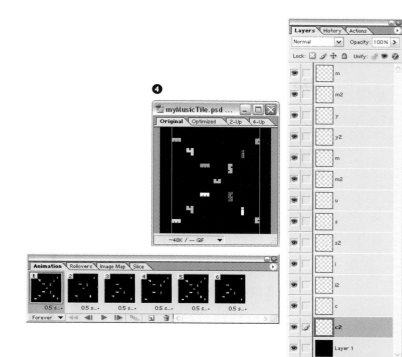

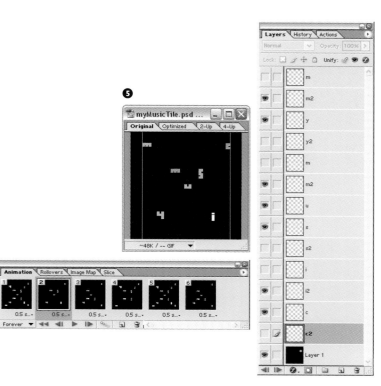

Every element of this animation is built on a 200 x 200 pixel module. You can use ImageReady to create these images. They do not require any visual effects, so there is no need to use Photoshop.

❶ Start by opening a new document, 200 x 200 pixels, and give it a black background. The text colour here is yellow RGB 252/232/0. The seven letters of the title 'myMusic' will span a diagonal to reach the bottom right of the document, with each letter positioned on a new layer. Here Minimum Noir Plafond was used, which has no curves, but you may prefer to draw your own letterforms. On a new layer create the first character letter 'm' at the top left, using the same font as the title.

❷ Continue adding letters on new layers until the title is complete.

❸ Now start again at the bottom left and add the title again. The layers panel should now look like this.

❹ It is this file that will form the background animation. Go to *Animation > New Frame* and repeat this until you have six frames. In frame 1 all the layers are visible.

❺ Click on frame 2 and select the layers that you want to be visible. Turn off the others.

64

6 Click on frame 3 and repeat the above process.

7 Do the same with frame 4 to repeat the process.

8 9 As above, do the same for frame 5 and then frame 6.

10 These are the six frames of the animation. In the *Animation* panel, set the *Frame Delay* to 0 seconds to match the fast tempo of the music clip that will accompany this animation.

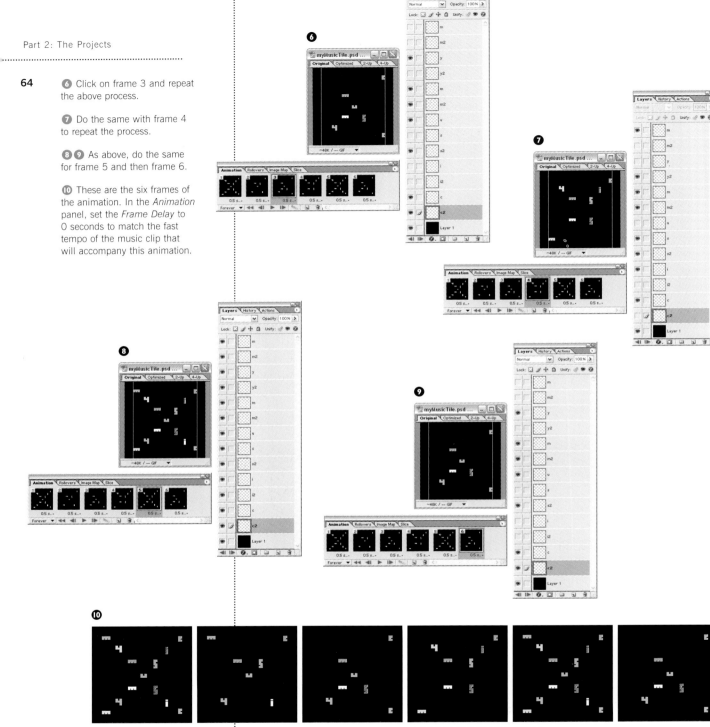

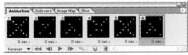

⑪ Now turn your attention to the second animation, the main title panel. Open another new document, sized 200 x 200 pixels, again with a black background. Paste in a suitable background image. (We used a silhouette of a man against some sheet music.)

⑫ Add a new layer and fill it with magenta, RGB 253/0/127. Go to *Layer Blending > **Multiply***. This will allow the layer underneath to shown through.

⑬ Create two more layers above and add the title 'myMusic' in the same font as before, making one layer magenta, and the other yellow.

⑭ From the *Animation* panel select *New Frame* again, and repeat this process until you have eight frames. In frame 1 select the layers to be visible.

⑮ Do the same for frame 2 and continue alternating the colourways until frame 8 is reached. Adjust the delay for the first four frames to 0.5 seconds. The other four frames have no delay – this will provide a counterpoint to the tempo of the background animation.

⑯ In the *Optimize* panel use most of the default settings for GIF, but reduce *Colours* to eight.

⑰ Now return to the document that you left at step ten and optimize it, setting *Colours* to nine this time. Use *File > **Save Optimized*** to save both animations.

66

⓲ You can now build the webpage. Using a Web design application – we've used Dreamweaver – make a six-frame frameset by dragging out frames from the border. Set the top row depth to 200 pixels and set the first two columns to a width of 200 pixels each. Place the cursor within each frame in turn. Go to *Modify > Page Properties > **Background Image*** to select the background animated GIF.

⓳ Continue this process until all six frames are filled with the background image. From the *Properties* panel select the bottom row of frames and set the *Row Value* to 1 and *Units* to *Relative*. This enables the bottom row to increase to any size when the browser is expanded, while the top row will stay at 200 pixels. All the frames should have the following settings selected: *No Borders, No Resize, No Scroll* and *Margins* set to *0*.

Remember, the frameset is a place holder that displays six individual HTML pages. Save each page and then save the frameset as index.htm if it is to be your website's homepage. If not, the name doesn't matter.

⓲
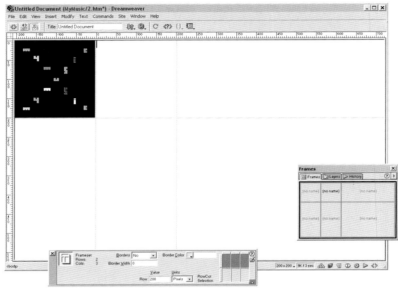

⓳
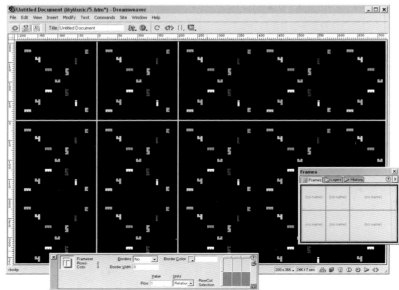

20

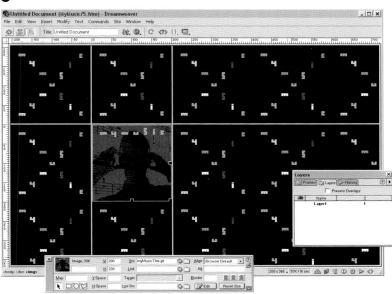

21

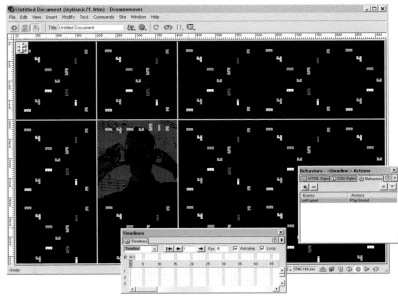

22

20 Click on *Objects > Layers* to create a new layer in the centre frame. Place the cursor within it and then use Insert Image to add the Title animation.

21 Place the cursor within the top left frame, then go to *Timeline > Add Behavior* to add the sound file. Also make sure you select *Autoplay*. Ensure that you use a sound file that has been edited to produce a seamless loop when repeated.

22 Finally, test the animation in your browser.

68 HEAVY HEAD

This project demonstrates three Flash features. First, *Tweening* – our character's face is drawn only twice, 'normal' and squashed, and *Shape Tweening* takes care of the in-between frames. ('Tweening' comes from 'in between'.) Second, all the images are vectors, which results in a file size of just 4kb. Third, control: the animation is user-initiated, beginning when the weight symbol is clicked.

The animation consists of 55 frames with four layers: Weight, Face, Button and Background, and each has been drawn directly in Flash. The weight image starts offstage and drops to its final position above the squashed face (*Motion Tweening* takes care of the in-between frames). The weight is copied and pasted to the button layer and reduced to a convenient size. The background is a flat yellow/green. The face remains unchanged for the first six frames while the weight is moving down.

When the weight makes contact, the head begins to be squashed. As is usually the case, it is easier to work back from the objects' final position in keyframe 12, then create the start positions for keyframe 1. The face shape and the individual features are each distorted individually to give a more convincing result.

TIP

There and back again

Actions can be applied to keyframes as well as to buttons so that an animation will return to the beginning once it has completed one cycle. Use the *Go To* action on frame 55 to reset to frame 1.

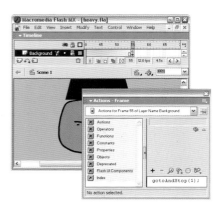

❶

❷

❸

❶ Fire up Flash and a new animation window will be generated. Select *Modify* > *Movie* > **Movie Properties** (in Flash MX select *Modify* > **Document**) to set your animation parameters. This animation uses the default settings, including the size 550 pixels x 400 pixels, so just click on *OK* in this panel.

❷ Use the '+' icon from the *Timeline* panel to add three extra layers. Name the layers 'Weight', 'Face', 'Button', and 'Background'.

❸ Select the *Rectangle* tool and make sure that *Stroke* is set to *Nil*, and *Fill* is set to RGB 204/204/51 (or Web colour CCCCFF). Go to the layer called Background and draw a rectangle to fill the stage area (550 x 400 pixels). The coordinates x:0, y:0 show that it is in the correct position. Click the dot in the layer's *Lock* column (within the Timeline) to avoid accidentally altering this.

❹ Now go to the Face layer and ensure *Stroke* is set to four pixels. (In Flash MX use the *Properties* window to do this.) Select *Object* > *Pencil* > *Options* > **Ink** (or *Options* > **Ink** in the Properties window in Flash MX). Draw the face shape and fill it with lilac, using RGB 204/204/255 (Web colour CCCC33). Pick the *Pencil* tool and draw the features.

❺ Now draw the weight itself on the Weight layer. For the circular handle, use the *Oval* tool, with *Stroke* set to ten pixels. For the main body of the weight, use the *Rectangle* tool with *Stroke* set to *Nil*. Refine the shape using the *Subselect* tool (the hollow arrow) from the *Tools* window. Use the *Visibility* column in the *Timeline* to hide or show layers as you work.

❻ Select the Weight image and go to *Insert* > **Convert to Symbol**. Name it 'Weight' and select *Graphic* as its *Behavior*. The symbol can now be reused.

70

⑦ Drag-select the frames in the *Timeline* for all your layers up to frame 54, and choose *Insert > Frame*. Then on the Face layer click in frame 6 and then 12, using *Insert > Keyframe* to add keyframes each time. At frame 12 select *Modify > Transform > Scale* so that handles appear around the object. Drag the centre top handle down until the face is squashed. Apply a darker colour fill to make the face look like it is under pressure – RGB 204/153/255 (Web colour CC99FF) is effective.

⑧ Click in the area between frames 6 and 12 and go to *Frame > Tweening > Shape*, or *Tween > Shape* from the Properties window in Flash MX. Click the *Onion Skin* button in the *Timeline* panel to see the effect of the *Shape Tween*.

⑨ Return to frame 1 of the Weight layer and move the Weight up so that it is just 'offstage'.

⑩ At frame 6 add a keyframe, and another instance of the Weight symbol automatically appears. Drag it down so that it is sitting on the face.

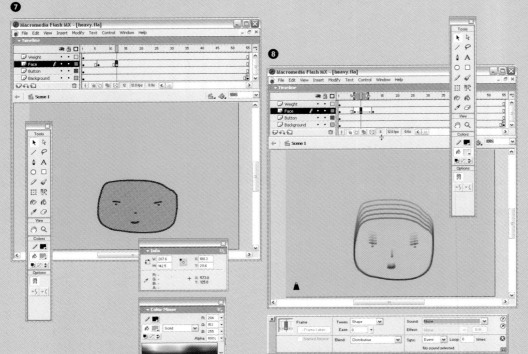

11 Repeat this entire process at frame 12.

12 Click in the area between frames 1 and 6, then select *Frame > Motion Tweening*, keeping the default values. In Flash MX choose *Tween > Motion* from the *Properties* window. Then click between frames 6 and 12 and repeat the process. The weight now automatically follows the squashed face.

13 Now copy the Weight image, return to the Button layer, and add a blank keyframe. Use *Transform* to reduce the image to a convenient size, and place it in the bottom left corner. Select *Insert > Convert to Symbol*, name it Weight and set the *Behavior* to *Button*. Add frames up to frame 55 if this hasn't already happened.

14 Now you can make the Weight button perform an action. With it selected, simply go to *Object Actions > '+' > Basic Actions > Play*. Flash MX users should pick *Actions > Movie Control > Play* from the Actions menu.

15 The panel shows that when the mouse is released the timeline will play.

16 The final task is to reset the animation after the button has been pressed. Make sure nothing is selected, then choose *Object Actions > '+' > Basic Actions > GoTo*. In Flash MX pick *Actions > Movie Control > GoTo* from the Actions window instead.

17 By default the *Action* will be *Play*, but you need to change this to *Stop*, since the Button will initiate *Play* in this project.

18 To do this, click the arrow in the bottom right and a further menu will be displayed. Deselect *Go To and Play*, and the *Action* will change to *Go To and Stop*. Flash MX users need simply click the *Go To and Stop* button.

19 The animation is now complete, so save it and go to *File > Export Movie* and give it a name. You will see that the film has a .swf file extension while the Flash file that you have been creating has a .fla extension.

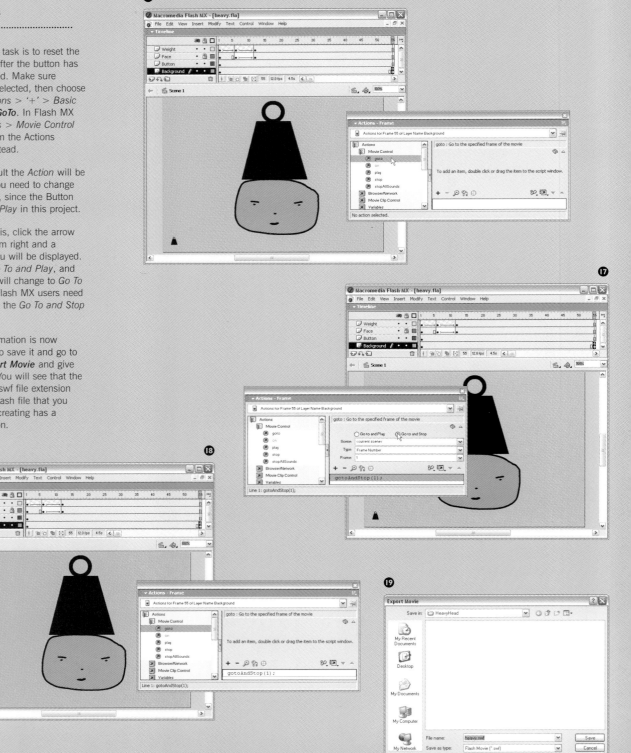

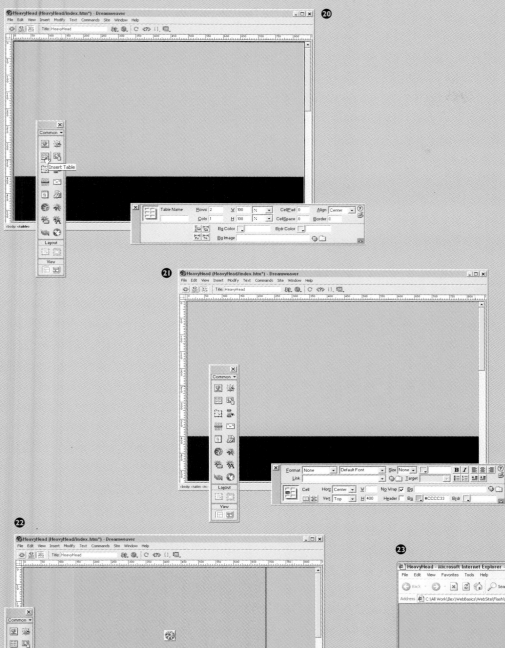

20 Finally it is time to place the Flash movie in a webpage. If you use Dreamweaver, select the *Objects* panel to create a table with two rows and one column, setting the *Width* and *Height* to 100 per cent. This will ensure the animation automatically fills any size of browser window.

21 Click in the upper cell/row of the table and from the *Properties* panel adjust *Horiz* to *Centre*, *Vert* to *Top*, *H* to *400*, select *No Wrap* and finally change *Bg* to the *Background* colour of the animation. (This is shown in Dreamweaver as a Hexidecimal value rather than RGB, but you can click the arrow to input RGB values.) Fill the lower cell/row with black.

22 Place the cursor in the top cell and use the *Objects* panel to insert the Flash movie. Finally, from *Page Properties* insert 0 as the value in the four *Margins* menus. (In other applications such as Freeway or GoLive, just insert the Flash movie using the appropriate methods.)

23 Now test your animation in your browser.

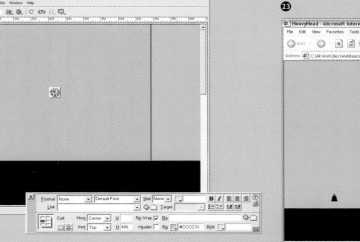

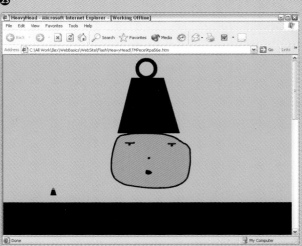

74 MY RESUMÉ

If you want to impress a future employer, how about using an animated CV or Resumé? This Flash example is lightweight enough to be e-mailed as well as to be used as a splash screen on your personal website. First off you will need some pictures of yourself. Unless you have access to a photographic studio, take them outdoors on a bright day, against the plainest background that you can find. Once scanned or downloaded from a digital camera, convert the background to white using a bitmap application like Photoshop.

The next step is to trace the bitmaps so that they can be converted to vectors. Flash has a trace function, but other specialist scanning applications such as CorelScan are more sophisticated. The idea is to reduce the bitmap to a number of discrete shapes of the same colour, then save them to a vector format that Flash can import, e.g. Freehand, Illustrator or EPS. The beauty of vector graphics, of course, is their scalability.

T I P

Shadow play

After you have traced a bitmap image, remove any unwanted areas from the vector image in order to simplify it and make it quicker to display. Sometimes small patches of white or shadows around the feet remain; these need to be removed if the image is above a background.

❸

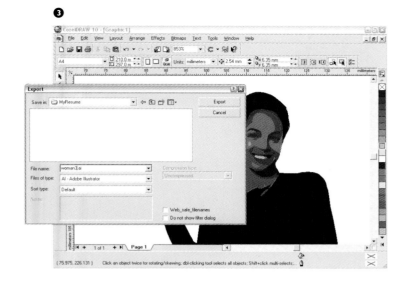

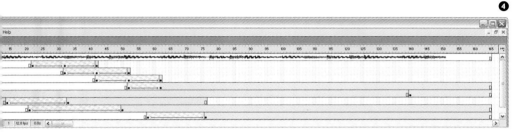

❹

❺

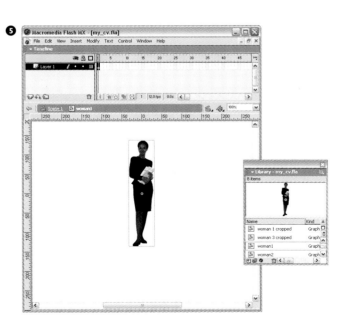

❶ Choose the photographs that you want to use for this animation and use a trace utility, such as CorelTrace, to convert the bitmaps into vector shapes. You can trace in Flash by choosing *Modify* > **Trace Bitmap**, but the level of control offered may not be enough. CorelTrace enables you to trace using various methods – the example here is *Outline*. Use the slider to set the appropriate level of accuracy.

❷ Open or copy and paste the image into a vector application, such as CorelDraw. Ungroup and remove the background, making any other necessary adjustments. (If your image backgrounds are not white, you may wish to retouch them in a bitmap application before tracing.)

❸ Export and save the images into a vector format that Flash will import such as .ai, .swf or .eps. (You can download a CorelDraw import filter from Macromedia for Flash if you require.)

❹ Open a new Flash document using the default settings. Create layers on the empty timeline. (The completed timeline is shown in all the screenshots for your reference.)

❺ Click *Library* > '+' > **Symbol**. We've called our image Woman1 – obviously, name your own appropriately. An empty *Library* window will appear, so go to *File* > **Import** and select the file to make the new image visible. Continue this process with the other three images.

76

❻ At frame 1 of the 'Woman 1' cropped layer, drag an instance of the first image onstage and use *Modify > Transform* to enlarge it. Create a new symbol and name it. Ours is called 'Woman1 Cropped'.

❼ Use the *Effects* panel to reduce the strength of the image. The *Advanced* menu was used in this example, but a simple reduction in Alpha transparency might be okay. It depends on the image you use.

❽ Add keyframes at frames 14 and 43. At frame 43 go to *Effects > Alpha Transparency* and change it to 0 per cent. (In Flash MX go to the *Properties* window and choose *Colour > Alpha*.) Next go to *Frame > Motion Tweening*, or *Tween > Motion* in Flash MX's *Properties* window, leaving the settings as they are.

❾ At frame 50 of Woman 3 Cropped layer (or your equivalent), repeat the process described in step 6, this time enlarging the image Woman 3. Drag the keyframe back to frame 21 and add another to replace it at frame 50. At frame 21 reduce the Alpha Transparency to 0 per cent.

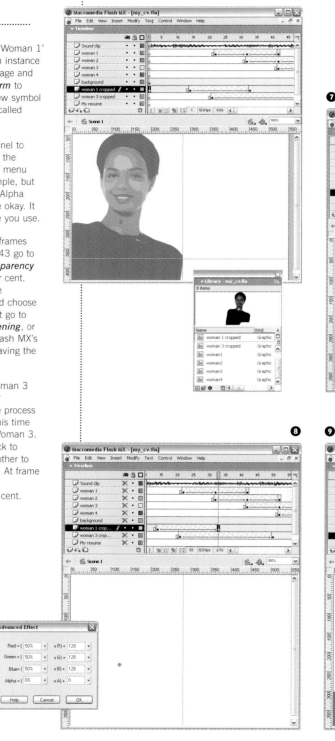

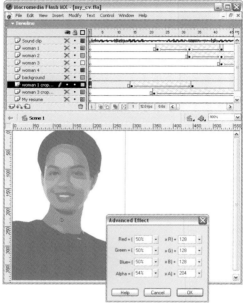

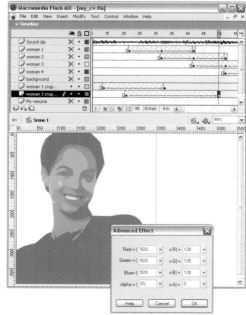

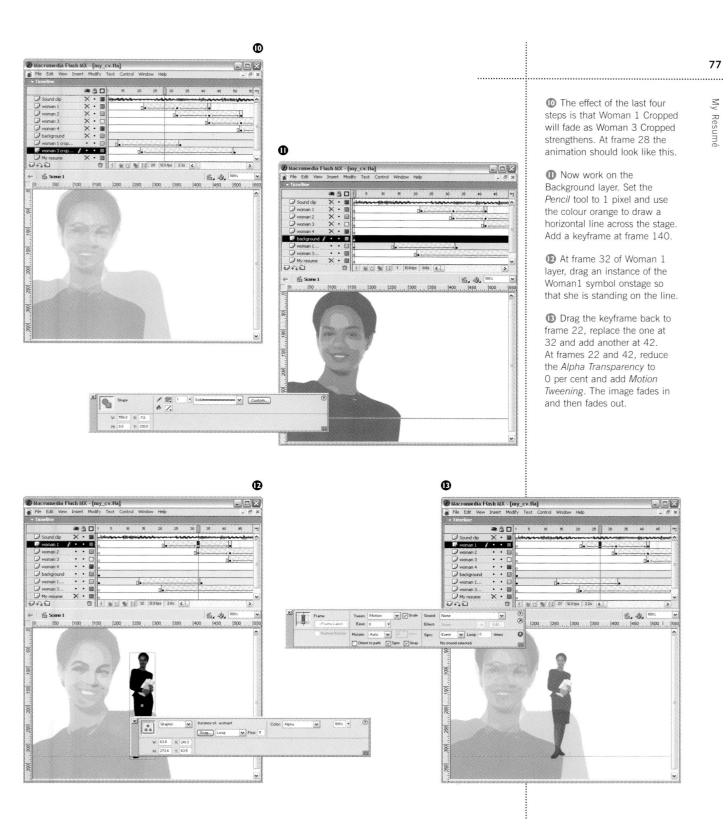

⑩ The effect of the last four steps is that Woman 1 Cropped will fade as Woman 3 Cropped strengthens. At frame 28 the animation should look like this.

⑪ Now work on the Background layer. Set the *Pencil* tool to 1 pixel and use the colour orange to draw a horizontal line across the stage. Add a keyframe at frame 140.

⑫ At frame 32 of Woman 1 layer, drag an instance of the Woman1 symbol onstage so that she is standing on the line.

⑬ Drag the keyframe back to frame 22, replace the one at 32 and add another at 42. At frames 22 and 42, reduce the *Alpha Transparency* to 0 per cent and add *Motion Tweening*. The image fades in and then fades out.

14 On the Woman 2 layer repeat the above process, centred on frame 42.

15 On the Woman 3 layer repeat the above process, centred on frame 52.

16 On the Woman 4 layer repeat the above process, centred on frame 62, but don't fade out again because this image persists until the end of the animation.

17 At frame 58 the images look like this.

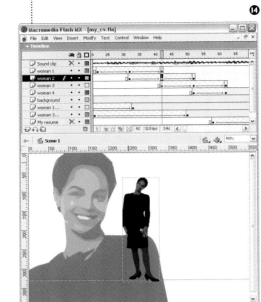

⑱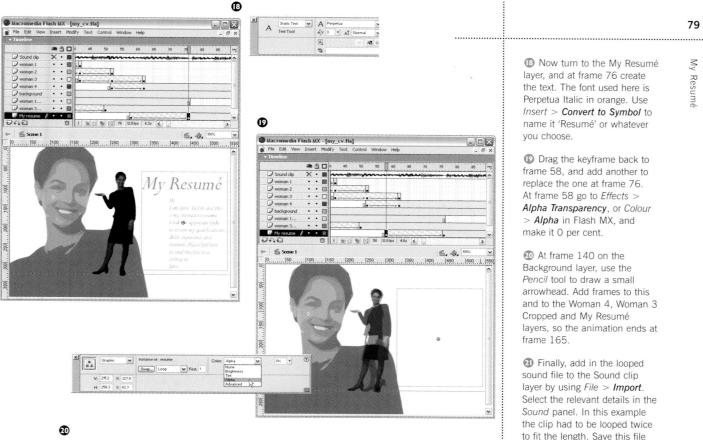

⑲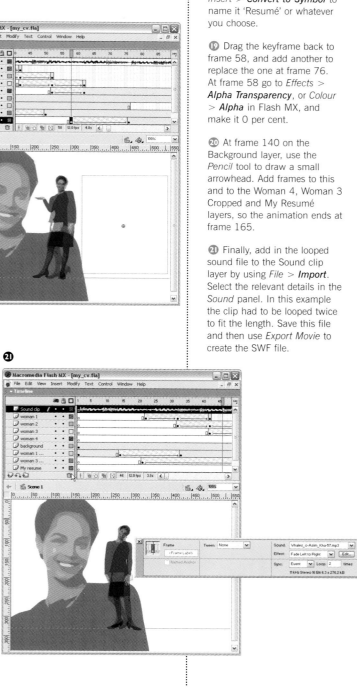

⑳

㉑

⑱ Now turn to the My Resumé layer, and at frame 76 create the text. The font used here is Perpetua Italic in orange. Use *Insert > Convert to Symbol* to name it 'Resumé' or whatever you choose.

⑲ Drag the keyframe back to frame 58, and add another to replace the one at frame 76. At frame 58 go to *Effects > Alpha Transparency*, or *Colour > Alpha* in Flash MX, and make it 0 per cent.

⑳ At frame 140 on the Background layer, use the *Pencil* tool to draw a small arrowhead. Add frames to this and to the Woman 4, Woman 3 Cropped and My Resumé layers, so the animation ends at frame 165.

㉑ Finally, add in the looped sound file to the Sound clip layer by using *File > Import*. Select the relevant details in the *Sound* panel. In this example the clip had to be looped twice to fit the length. Save this file and then use *Export Movie* to create the SWF file.

80 CUSTOM AUTO COLOUR

This project demonstrates once again how small an all-vector Flash animation can be: this one is just 13kb! Create the original car image in a vector application – we used CorelDraw. (You could, alternatively, use clip art.) The image needs to be separated into parts so that each can be exported as an EPS file; these can then be imported into Flash and placed on separate layers.

Two important features are exploited here, the reuse of symbols, and interactivity (ie user controls). The imported image parts are first converted to individual symbols. This enables an Instance to be created by inserting a new keyframe on each of the layers that will change during animation. Each Instance's shape, colour and position can then be edited without changing the original symbol stored in the *Library*.

To enable each paint colour to be applied to the car body, a sequence of keyframes is created, and each Instance of the symbol 'Car Two-tone' is amended to include the new colour. Each colour panel in the *Control Colours* layer is also saved as a symbol but this time as a button, which enables an action to be associated with it. At the end of each sequence a *Stop* action is applied to the final frame. For Button six, the sequence is extended so that a driver appears at the wheel and the car speeds off.

TIP

Simulating glass with Transparency

The shape of the car windshield was repeated and saved as a symbol in a new layer. This allows *Alpha Transparency* to be applied after a white/blue linear blend is used as a fill. This gives a translucent effect simulating glass.

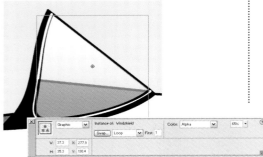

❶

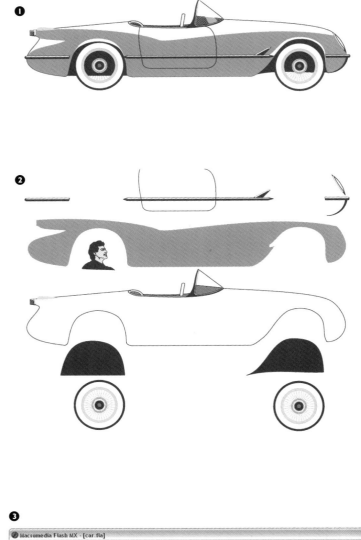

❷

❸

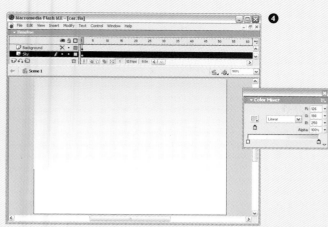

① Select a car graphic to use in this animation. Whatever you pick, it must be a vector image so that it can be deconstructed.

② Use an application such as CorelDraw to separate the image into the component parts you will use in Flash. Here we've made a few minor colour modifications, and added a clip-art driver to the image collection. Export each item as an EPS with a transparent background.

③ Take a moment to study the timeline of this animation. The various components of the car appear as separate layers. The stacking order is important because those on the top obscure those beneath. The car starts with a cream paint job; the 'Car Two-tone' layer contains colour options that are triggered by clicking *Control Colours* (the coloured buttons at the bottom). A separate layer below contains the *Actions* required to do this. The Sky appears at the bottom of the layers since it is behind everything else. The Background is the black area, which also contains the white title. At the very top of the layers is the blue Title that makes a brief appearance towards the end of the animation. Finally, there is an extra refinement that did not exist in the imported images: the transparent Windshield (see our Tip, *opposite*).

④ Now you need to turn off the layer visibility for the layers that are not being used, and recreate them one by one. In each case, click in frame 1 of the layer and start creating – a keyframe symbol will then automatically appear. Start with the Sky and use the *Fill* panel to select a *Linear Gradient*, then draw the sky area with the *Rectangle* tool.

⑤ On the Background layer create the black panel and add the text in white. Here, the font Lewinsky was chosen because it echoes the 'Fifties' character of the car.

⑥ On the Car body layer, go to *File > Import* to add the image. Use the *Insert > Convert to Symbol* and name it 'Car Body'. (Each remaining imported image must also be converted to a symbol using *Graphic* as the *Behavior*.)

⑦ On the Car wheel arches layer, add the relevant image in the same way.

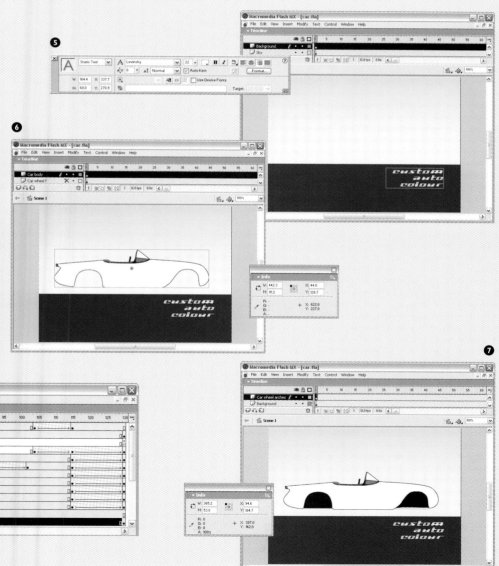

82

⑧ Add in the wheel images on the Car Wheel F and B layers. If the car doesn't sit comfortably on the top of the black area, lower the last three layers so that it does.

⑨ Add the appropriate image on the Car Trim layer.

⑩ On the Windshield layer select the *Linear Gradient Fill* and use the *Colour Mixer* to set it from white to pale blue. Then use the *Pen* tool to draw a shape that will exactly cover the windshield. Use the *Transform* Fill tool to rotate the fill. Finally, go to *Insert > Convert to Symbol* and name it 'Windshield'. The enlarged view here is shown in *Library* mode.

⑪ Return to Scene 1 mode and select *Effects > Alpha Transparency*, or *Colour > Alpha* in Flash MX, and make it 65 per cent.

⑫ On *Layer Control Colours* use the *Oval* tool to create two circles, one for each end of the rounded end of the panel. Then draw a rectangle to fill the space in between, ensuring that *Stroke* is set to *Nil* before you start.

⑬ Use *Insert > Convert to Symbol > Behavior > Button* and name this 'Button 1'. Continue repeating this process until you have created six buttons and saved each as a symbol.

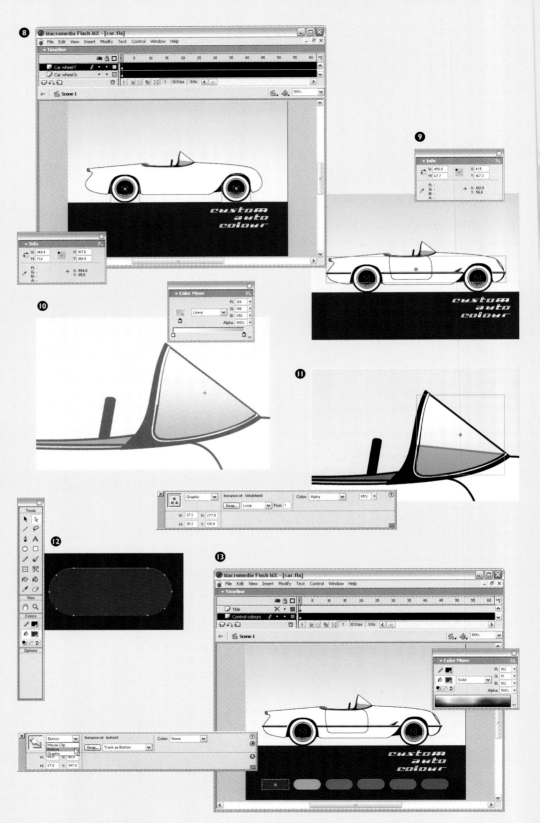

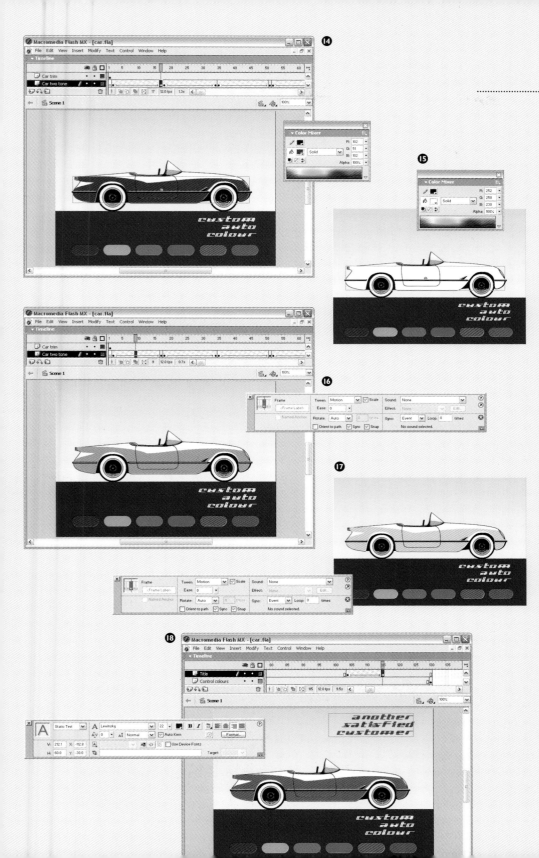

14 On the Car Two-tone layer add the relevant image and convert it to a graphic. Drag the resulting keyframe to frame 2 on the *Timeline*. This gives you your first view of the car without the two-tone enhancement. Add another keyframe at frame 17 and from *Effect > Tint* (or *Colour > Tint* from the *Properties* window in Flash MX) select a colour that matches Button 1.

15 Return to frame 2 and, using the *Tint* option again, select a cream colour that exactly matches the car body colour.

16 Click between frame 2 and 17 and add *Frame > Motion Tweening*, (or *Tween > Motion* in Flash MX), using the default settings. At this midway position in the Tween, you can see that the colour is changing from cream to purple.

17 Continue this process of adding pairs of keyframes with 16 frames between them, applying colours to match the buttons and adding *Motion Tweening* until all six colours are complete.

18 Now move ahead to the Title layer and frame 104. Create the title text in dark blue, convert it to a graphic and name it Title. Add a new keyframe at frame 115. At frame 104, reduce *Alpha Transparency* to 0 per cent, then click between the two frames and add *Frame > Motion Tweening*, or *Tween > Motion* in the *Properties* window in Flash MX, keeping the default settings.

⑲ On the Car Man layer at frame 104, use *File > Import* again to add the image. Go to *Insert > Convert to Symbol > Behavior > Graphic* and name it 'Man'. All the elements that have been imported or created are now in the *Library*, which should look like this. Add a new keyframe at 115. At frame 104 reduce *Alpha Transparency* to 0 per cent, then click in between the two frames and add *Motion Tweening*.

⑳ Add another keyframe at frame 130 and then proceed to add keyframes at this position to all the Car layers, plus the Windshield layer. Select all the images on these and move the car offstage to the right.

㉑ Between frames 115 and 130 on all relevant layers, use *Frame > Effect > Motion Tweening*, or *Tween > Motion* in the Properties window in Flash MX. Keep most of the default settings, changing only Ease to −100 so the tween starts slowly and then accelerates towards the end.

㉒ The content of the animation is now in place. What you need to do now is control events using *Actions*. On *Layer Control Colours* click on the first button and select *Frame Actions > '+' > Basic Actions > On Mouse Event*. In Flash MX, go to the Actions window and select *Actions > Movie Control > On*. The default setting should be 'On Release', so select *GoTo* to insert a *GotoAndPlay(1) Action*. Change the *Frame* here from 1 to 2. Now when the first button is clicked and released the animation will move to frame 2 and play. Then you need to make the other five buttons play their appropriate frames.

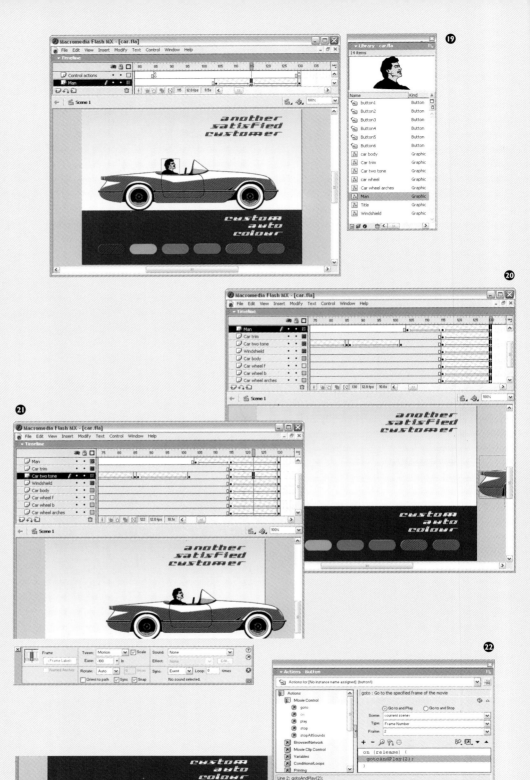

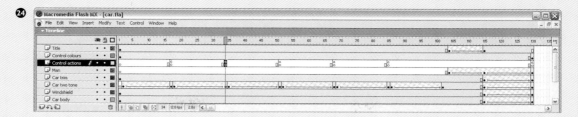

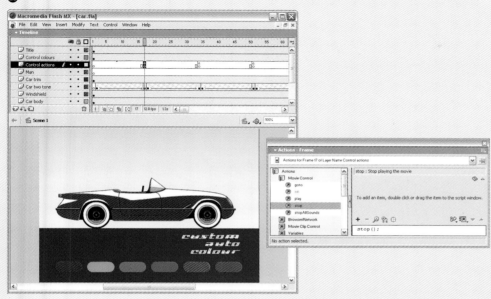

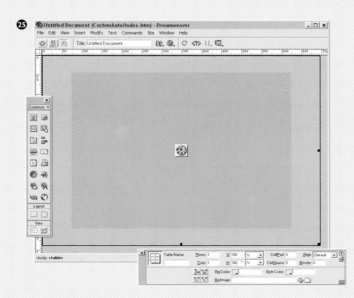

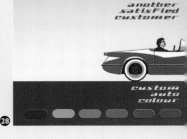

85

Custom Auto Colour

23 On the Layer Control Actions at frame 17, insert a blank keyframe. Select *Frame Actions > '+' > Basic Actions > Stop*. (*Actions > Movie Control > Stop* in MX.)

24 Repeat this process at frames 34, 51, 68 and 85 but not at frame 102. This is the point at which the final two-tone colour appears (a couple of frames after this, the 'satisfied customer' title appears and the car zooms offstage to the right). So the final Stop action is applied to frame 130. The animation is complete, so save it and go to *File > Export Movie*.

25 In Dreamweaver create a table that has 100 per cent Width and 100 per cent Height so that it always fills the browser window. Inset the SWF image you have just created – it will appear as a grey placeholder with a Flash icon.

26 Click in the space between the image and the edge of the table and set Horiz to Centre and Vert to Middle to ensure that the animation always appears in the middle of the browser window.

27 Remember to click on the SWF image and ensure that Loop and Autoplay are not selected in the Properties panel.

29 Now test this animation in your browser.

86 SAM'S SITE

This is a Flash header that you can use for your personal webpage. You know by now that an all-vector Flash animation is small and scalable, so although your animation will be created at 770 x 246 pixels, the HTML page is created so that the size of your Flash animation will vary. The animation is placed at the top of the page and its size set to 100 per cent of the browser width and 33.3 per cent of its depth. Whatever size the browser is dragged to, the animation will follow those proportions. When the aspect ratio is changed from the original 5.5:4.0, the text will become slightly distorted – the purist typographer may scoff, but we can bend the rules a little for this project.

The other key feature is colour change. Flash is brilliant at blending colours, and it is simple to do. The colours chosen for each piece of text or even for the background gradient hardly matter – as long as each item is converted to a symbol, then each Instance can have a different colour value. Add *Motion Tweening* between each *Instance* and the result will be a smooth transition from colour to colour. A word of warning: although vector Flash files download quickly, the processor on your PC or Mac has to do a lot of maths to interpret these changes on the fly. As a result, the animation will run slowly on a computer with a slow processor.

TIP

Going to the films

The vertical lines that whizz left and right on this animation are akin to the patterns you sometimes see on very old films, and add visual interest. They are on two separate layers so that the two lines do not follow the exactly the same path.

❶

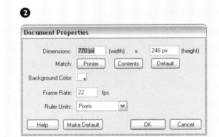

❷

❸

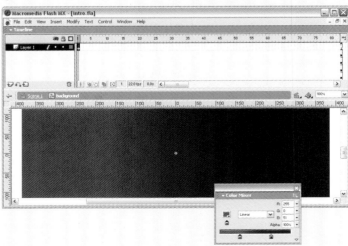

❶ The animation is split into two scenes. The first contains four visual layers: the background, the animation name (we've called ours 'Sam's Site') and the two line layers. It also has a layer for a sound file. The second scene starts as an identical copy of the first, with five layers added to provide the subject themes, such as Music, etc. The completed timelines for both scenes are shown here, so take a look at them before you start creating your own version.

❷ Go to *Modify* > **Movie Properties**, or *Modify* > **Document** in Flash MX, and change the dimensions to 770 pixels x 246 pixels and the frame rate to 22. You can experiment with changing the frame rates at any time.

❸ First create a background. Go to the *Library* window and click '+' to create a new *Symbol*. Call it 'Background'. Use the *Rectangle* tool, with *Stroke* set to *Nil*, to draw a shape that covers the stage (770 x 246 pixels). Use a *Gradient Fill* (red to blue in this example), and drag the sliders in a bit so that there is an area of solid colour at each end.

❹ At frame 1 on the Background layer, drag an instance of the Background symbol onstage so that it covers the entire area.

❺ At frame 10 add a keyframe and use the *Effects* > **Advanced** option, or *Colour* > **Advanced** in Flash MX, to change the background graphic colour. Add two more keyframes on this layer, changing the colour each time, and finally add one more at the last frame, 83. The colour here must be identical to that in frame 1. The first and last keyframes of the Background layer in both scenes should have the same colour values, so that the transition between them is smooth. Click in the area between each set of keyframes and select *Frame* > **Motion Tweening**, or *Tween* > **Motion** in Flash MX.

❹

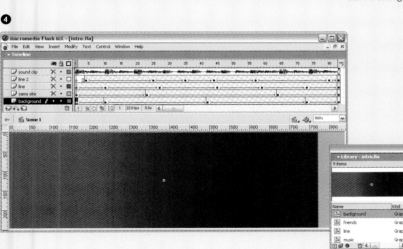

❺

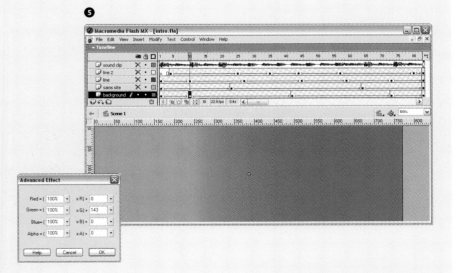

6 Now move on to the Sam's Site layer. Create the text for this using your preferred font and colour – the M and S are overlapped in our example. To do this, use *Modify* > **Break Apart**. Then go to *Insert* > **Convert to Symbol** and name it 'Sam's Site'. Make the white text semitransparent by going to *Effects* > **Alpha Transparency**, or *Colour* > **Alpha** in Flash MX, and changing it to 29 per cent.

7 At frames 23 and 64 add keyframes and alter the colours. Finally, add one more keyframe at the last frame, 83, making the colour here identical to that in frame 1. Click in the area between each set of keyframes and add *Motion Tweening* with its default values.

8 At frame 1 on the Line layer, use the *Line* tool set to 1 pixel to draw a vertical line that fills the stage. (A yellow line was used in the example). Convert this into a symbol and name it 'Line'. Make it semitransparent by setting the Alpha transparency value to 40 per cent. Next, add keyframes at various intervals, each time moving the Line left or right to a new position. Move to the Line 2 layer and repeat the process to make lines in different positions. Click in the area between each set of keyframes and add *Motion Tweening* with its default values once again.

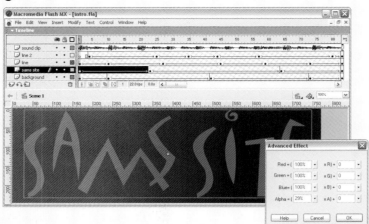

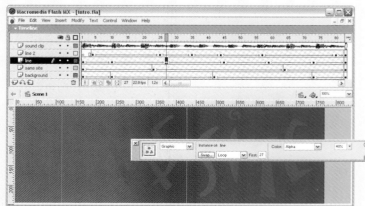

⑨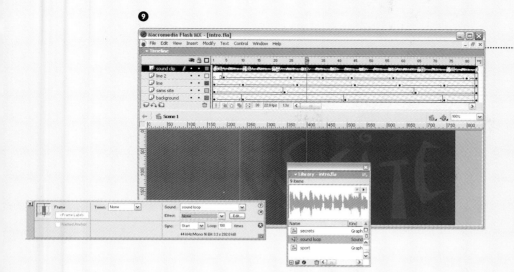

⑩

⑪

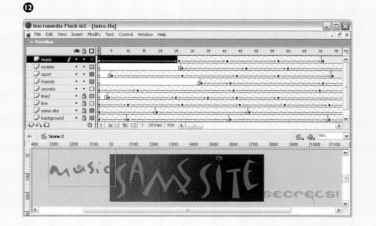

⑫

⑨ The last thing to do on this scene occurs at frame 1. On the Sound Clip layer use the *File* menu to import a sound clip. It must be a looped sound so that it repeats seamlessly. Imported sound files are automatically added to the *Library*.

⑩ Sound clips can be large – the one used in the example was 286kb in WAV format, before it was imported. Fortunately, Flash can resample and compress sound files. This one is now less than 7kb.

⑪ Now move on to scene 2. Use *Modify > Scene > '+'* to add scene 2. You can move back and forth between scenes by clicking the icon at the bottom right of the timeline.

⑫ In the *Edit* menu, choose *Select All Frames*, then *Copy Frames*. Next step to scene 2 and choose *Paste Frames* to add all of the layers that appeared in scene 1, except the sound clip layer. Now add a further five layers above, naming them with the words that you wish to animate. The screenshot shows the animation image at 50 per cent.

90

⓭ Create each word in your preferred font and colour and use *Insert > Convert to Symbol*, naming each one the same as the layers. If you download the FLA file from our website, you can simply replace the words used there with your own selection.

⓮ Add three to five keyframes to each layer and move the words left or right. Only the Music and Secrets layers start at frame 1; the others are staggered. This sequence, taken at 15 frame intervals, shows the effect. The grey area is offstage and will not be visible in the final animation.

⓯ Add *Motion Tweening* between keyframes and use *Modify > Frame > Easing* (or the *Ease* control in Flash MX's *Properties* window) to add acceleration or deceleration to some of the tweens. This will add to the effect of chaotic movement. The animation is now complete, so save it and go to *File > Export Movie*.

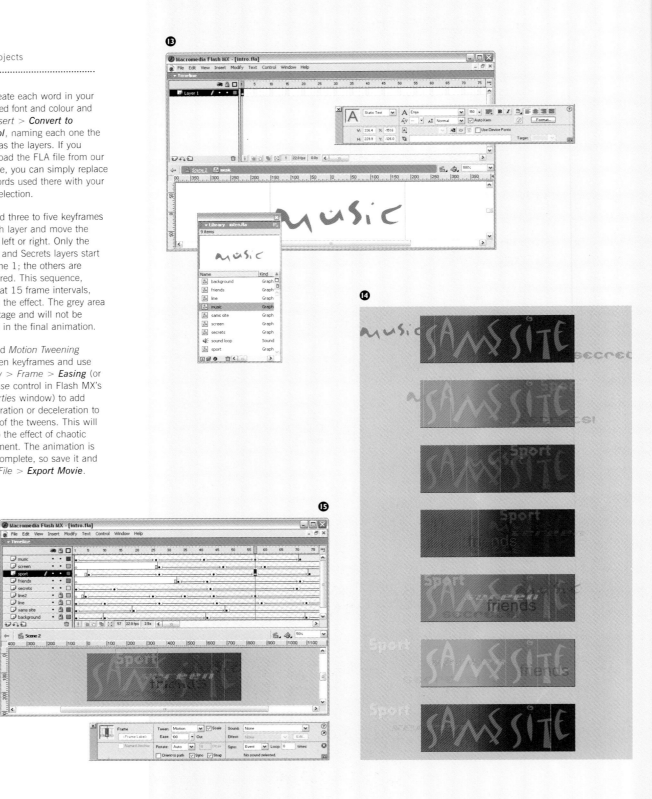

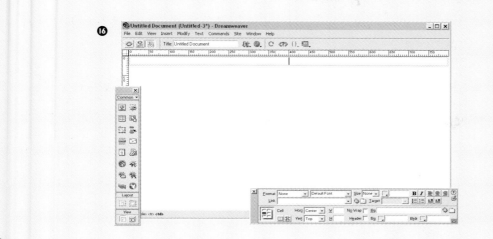

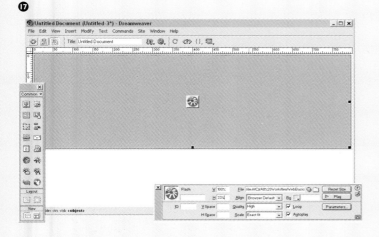

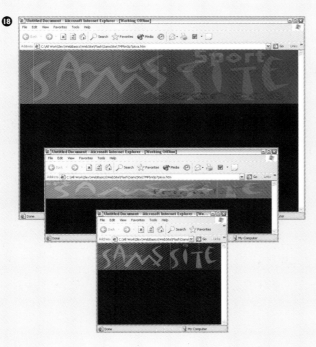

16 Now open Dreamweaver (or your equivalent) and create a table with *W* 100 per cent and *H* 100 per cent so that it will always fill the browser window. Click within the table and in the *Properties* panel change *Horiz* to *Center* and *Vert* to *Top*. Go to *Modify > **Page Properties*** to change all the margins to 0. Add a background colour to the page if you wish.

17 Insert the SWF image that you have just created – it will appear as a grey placeholder with just the Flash icon to identify it. In the *Properties* panel, change *W* to 100 per cent, *H* to 33 per cent, *Align* to *Top* and *Scale* to *Exact Fit*. *Loop* and *Autoplay* should already be selected. (If you prefer different Web page design tools, use the appropriate methods for inserting and controlling Flash movies.)

18 Now test your animation in your browser. As you can see, whatever its shape or size the animation will always occupy the top 33 per cent of the window.

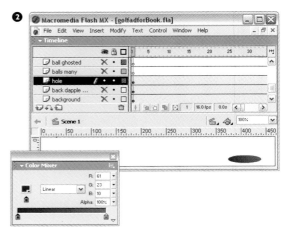

GOLFER'S PARADISE

The ubiquitous banner ad, seen on countless
websites, has traditionally been created in animated
GIF format. However, this one is made in Flash. It
exploits one of the quintessential features of Flash:
the Motion Tweening technique called Easing. This
allows the ball to slow down as it crosses the screen,
leaving just enough momentum to drop into the
'hole'. To enhance the effect of movement, you can
create a trailing, 'ghost' image; a second ball travels
one frame behind, on the layer below, reduced from
full strength to an Alpha value of 25 per cent. For
most of the animation, the ball has to appear in front
of the green background, but as it drops down into
the 'hole' it has to pass behind the green background.
To do this you need two background layers – a
complete one below the ball and another, partially
cut away, in front of it. The keyframes on each layer
must be staggered so that the action is properly
synchronized; the text appears and disappears just
as the ball travels across the screen. At the finale,
the eye is drawn to the ball partially bouncing out of
the 'hole' and to the 'Tell Me More' link.

TIP

Shadows and light

A tiny shadow travels along beneath the ball.
Although only 30 pixels wide, it makes the
animation much more convincing. It is a radial
gradient made from black to green, with the
green having a 0 per cent *Alpha* value.

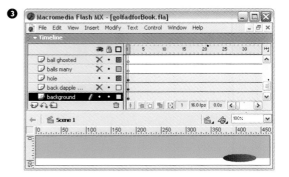

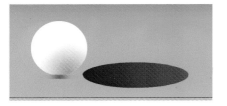

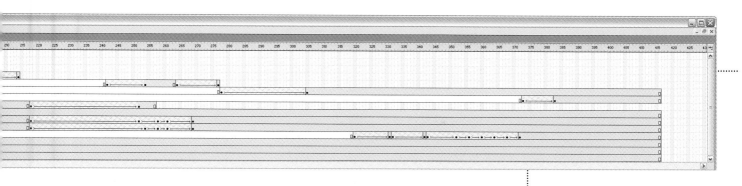

① Go to *Modify* > **Movie Properties**, or *Modify* > **Document** in Flash MX, to change the dimensions to 468 pixels x 60 pixels, which is the standard format for a banner ad. With 15 layers and 416 frames the timeline appears complex, but when it is broken down it becomes less formidable. Seven layers are created for the text messages that appear in sequence, a further three are for the balls, one is for the ball shadows, three are for the backgrounds, and one is for the 'hole'. Create these layers on the empty timeline. The completed timeline is shown in all the screenshots for you to refer to.

② The first task is to go to the Hole layer and draw an ellipse with the *Oval* tool, making sure *Stroke* is set to *Nil* and using a *Gradient Fill* of two shades of brown (putting the darker on the left).

③ On the Background layer, which must be at the bottom of the stacking order, use the *Rectangle* tool to create a green rectangle that extends down to the middle of the hole.

④ On the Background 2 layer, create another green rectangle with a cut-away semi–oval that corresponds to the Hole layer. (The previous two layers have been turned off to show this.)

⑤ On the top layer add a keyframe at frame 31 and add the text 'You're Serious about Golf' in dark brown or a colour of your choice, using the *Character* panel to specify font details. Use *Insert* > **Convert to Symbol** and name it 'You're serious'. Drag the keyframe back to frame 8 and replace it with another at frame 31.

6 At frame 8 go to *Effects > Alpha Transparency*, or *Colour > Alpha* in Flash MX, and change this to 0 per cent. Click in the area between these keyframes and choose *Frame > Motion Tweening*, or in Flash MX choose *Tween > Motion* from the *Properties* window, keeping the default settings.

7 At frames 47 and 62 add keyframes; at 62 reduce the Alpha transparency to 0 per cent and add *Motion Tweening*.

To recap on what has happened so far: the text first appears at frame 8 at 0 per cent, tweens to frame 31 where is it at 100 per cent, remains like this until frame 47 when, using the second tween, it begins its descent to frame 62 where it is again at 0 per cent. Continue this process with the remaining six layers of text.

8 On the 'It's not just' layer, repeat the process at frames 97 and 166, 126 and 140.

9 On the 'It's not even' layer, repeat the process at frames 140 and 154, 163 and 177.

10 On the 'It's an obsession' layer, repeat the process at frames 177, 192, 202 and 214.

11 On the 'So go ahead' layer, repeat the process at frames 242, 254, 264 and 277.

12 On the 'At golfers' layer, repeat the process at frames 278 and 305. This text persists until the end so there is no need for the second pair of keyframes.

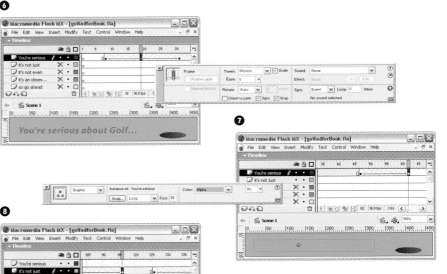

⑬

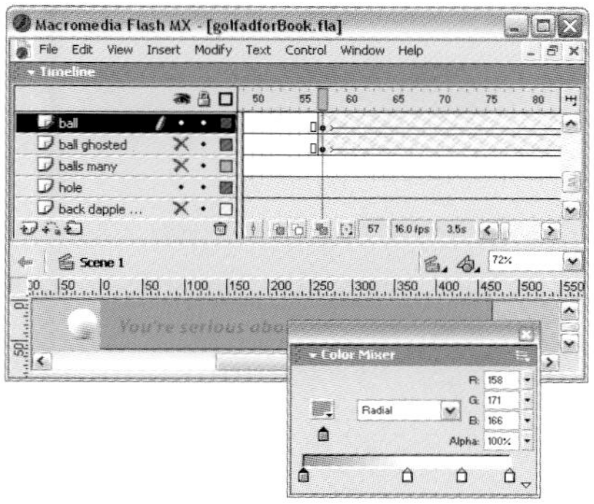

⑭

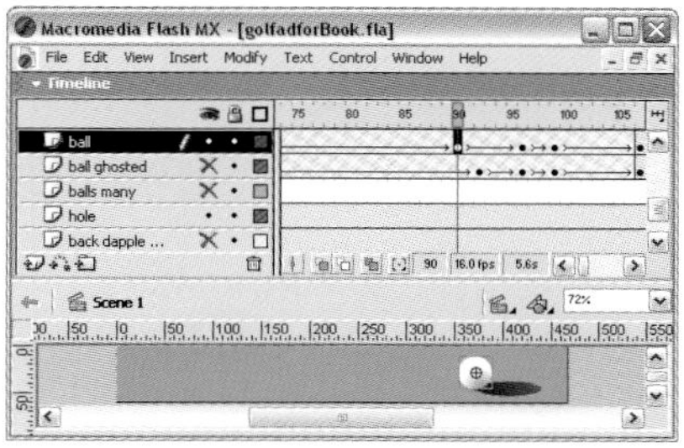

⑮

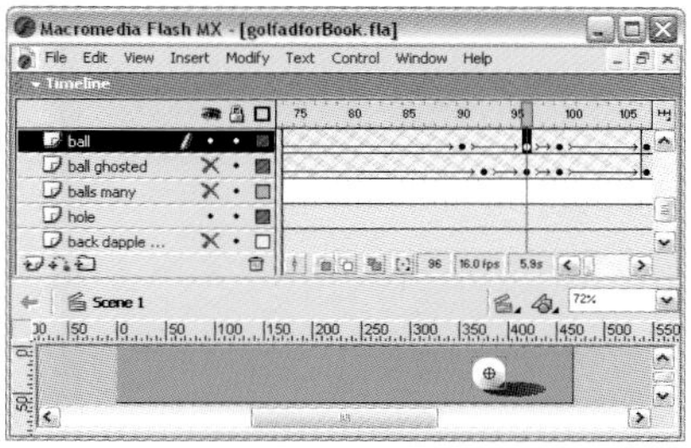

⑯

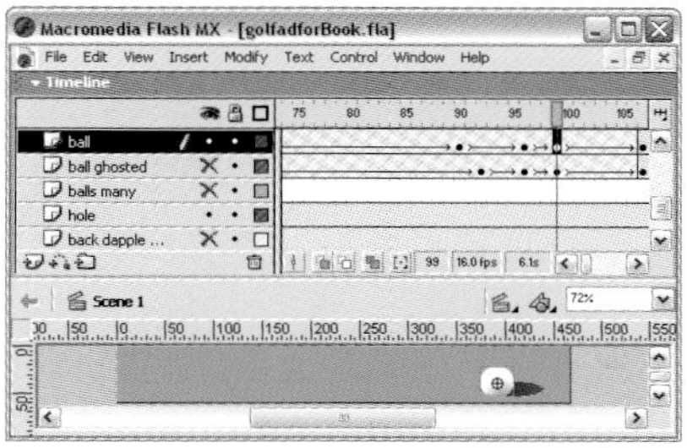

⑰

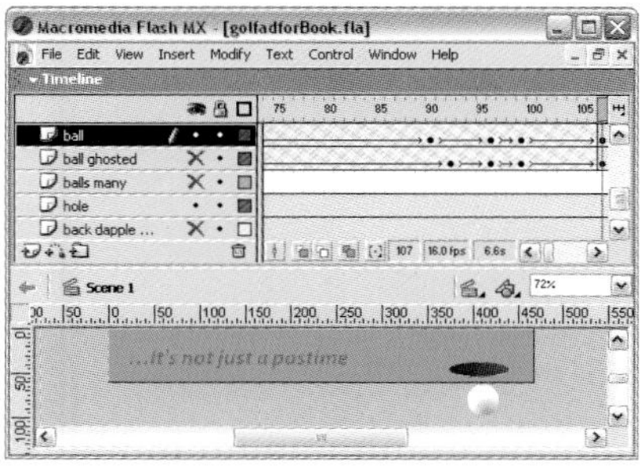

⑱

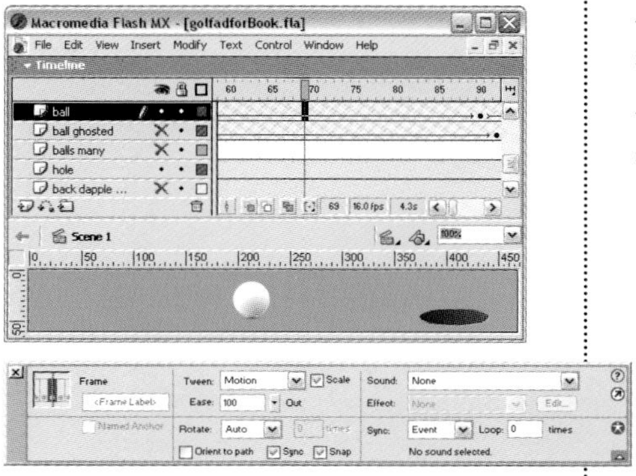

⑲

⑬ Now turn your attention to the ball. On the Ball layer, add a blank keyframe at frame 57. Using the *Oval* tool, with *Stroke* set to *Nil* and *Radial Gradient Fill* set from grey to white, draw the ball. Use the *Fill Transform* tool to rotate the fill anti-clockwise a little. Drag the ball offstage to the left.

⑭ Add another keyframe at frame 90 and drag the ball to the new position.

⑮ Add another keyframe at frame 96 and drag the ball to the new position.

⑯ Add another keyframe at frame 99 and drag the ball to the new position.

⑰ Add another keyframe at frame 107 and drag the ball to the new position.

⑱ Now add *Motion Tweening* between all these keyframes at its default settings. Between frames 57 and 90, which is where the ball slows almost to a stop at the hole, change *Easing* to 100.

⑲ The ball replicates these last five steps later in the animation so repeat the process at frames 218, 252, 258, 261 and 269. Turn the *Onion Skin* view on to see what is happening.

96

20 Now work on the ghosted ball. On frame 57 of the Ball Ghosted layer, add a blank keyframe. From the *Library* panel drag an instance of the ball onstage and position it exactly as it is in the Ball layer at frame 57. Go to *Effects > Alpha Transparency*, or *Colour > Alpha* in Flash MX's *Properties* window, and make it 17 per cent. Add another keyframe at frame 92 and position it exactly as the ball was at frame 90.

21 The ghosted ball has taken two extra frames to travel the same distance as the solid ball, so it will lag progressively behind during the course of its travel. To enable it to travel, you must of course apply *Motion Tweening*, using *Easing* at 100. Add additional keyframes at 96, 99 and 107 and apply *Motion Tweening* at its default settings this time.

22 The ghosted ball replicates these last five steps later in the animation, so repeat the process between frames 218 and 269. The ghosted ball is now hidden – it is behind the solid ball as it follows it down the hole.

23 Next to the Ball Shadow layer, add a blank keyframe on frame 57 and draw the flattened oval shape using the *Oval* tool set to *Nil* stroke then fill it with a *Radial Gradient* made from black to green. Give the green a 0 per cent Alpha value. Use *Insert > Convert to Symbol* and name it 'Ball Shadow'. Position it below the ball (just offstage left).

24 Add a keyframe at frame 90 and drag this shadow so it is under the ball. *Apply Motion Tweening* with *Easing* at 100.

20

21

22

23

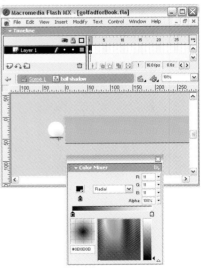

24

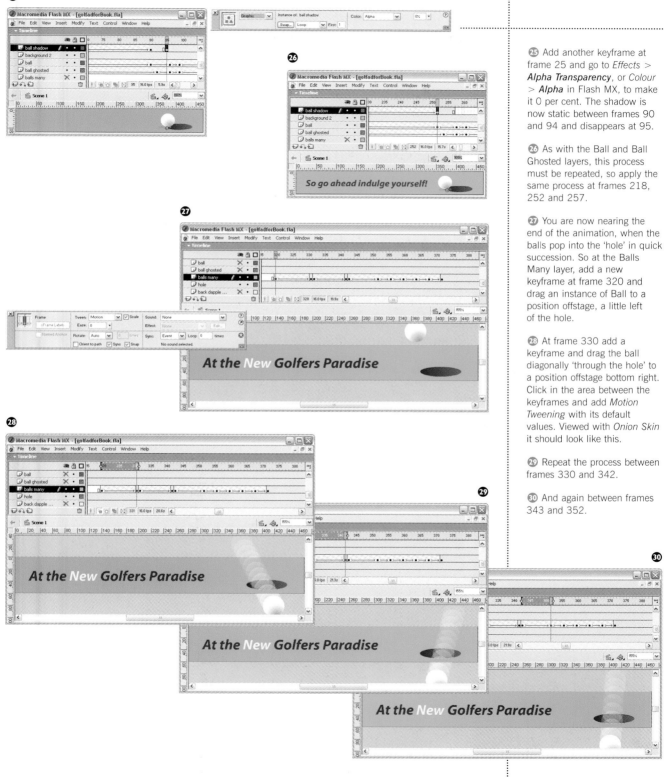

25 Add another keyframe at frame 25 and go to *Effects > Alpha Transparency*, or *Colour > Alpha* in Flash MX, to make it 0 per cent. The shadow is now static between frames 90 and 94 and disappears at 95.

26 As with the Ball and Ball Ghosted layers, this process must be repeated, so apply the same process at frames 218, 252 and 257.

27 You are now nearing the end of the animation, when the balls pop into the 'hole' in quick succession. So at the Balls Many layer, add a new keyframe at frame 320 and drag an instance of Ball to a position offstage, a little left of the hole.

28 At frame 330 add a keyframe and drag the ball diagonally 'through the hole' to a position offstage bottom right. Click in the area between the keyframes and add *Motion Tweening* with its default values. Viewed with *Onion Skin* it should look like this.

29 Repeat the process between frames 330 and 342.

30 And again between frames 343 and 352.

98

31 The final ball pops up again, indicating that the 'hole' is full of balls. This is achieved between frames 352 and 372, so add keyframes with *Motion Tweening*. Between 352 and 356 the ball moves upwards so set *Easing* to 100.

32 Between 356 and 360 the ball moves downwards, so use the default settings.

33 Between 360 and 364 the ball moves upwards. Set *Easing* to 57.

34 Between 364 and 368 the ball moves downwards, so use the default settings.

35 Between 368 and 372 the ball moves upwards. Use the default settings!

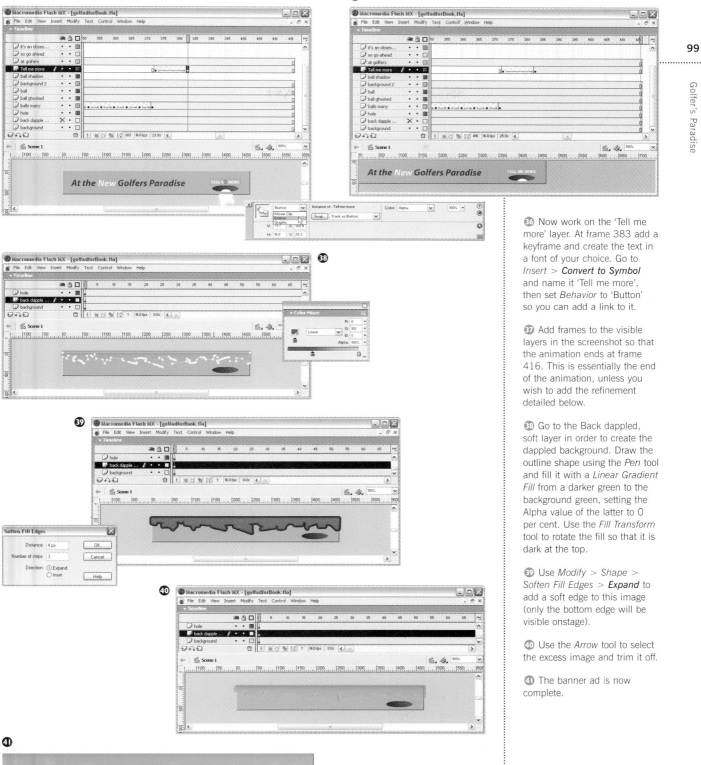

36 Now work on the 'Tell me more' layer. At frame 383 add a keyframe and create the text in a font of your choice. Go to *Insert* > **Convert to Symbol** and name it 'Tell me more', then set *Behavior* to 'Button' so you can add a link to it.

37 Add frames to the visible layers in the screenshot so that the animation ends at frame 416. This is essentially the end of the animation, unless you wish to add the refinement detailed below.

38 Go to the Back dappled, soft layer in order to create the dappled background. Draw the outline shape using the *Pen* tool and fill it with a *Linear Gradient Fill* from a darker green to the background green, setting the Alpha value of the latter to 0 per cent. Use the *Fill Transform* tool to rotate the fill so that it is dark at the top.

39 Use *Modify* > *Shape* > *Soften Fill Edges* > **Expand** to add a soft edge to this image (only the bottom edge will be visible onstage).

40 Use the *Arrow* tool to select the excess image and trim it off.

41 The banner ad is now complete.

100 DAVE'S FLYING CIRCUS

As this project demonstrates, Flash is just as adept at working with bitmaps as it is with vector images. However, the downside is file size: this one is a whopping 116kb! The bitmaps are images scanned into Photoshop as greyscale, and then the colour has been applied in Flash.

To begin this project, create a new document in Photoshop, or any other bitmap application. It should be the same size as the animation, and at 72 dpi. Scan the images at a higher dpi to capture more detail, paste them into the master document and reduce them to fit. To enable the figures to move around the animation space and to appear behind a window, for example, the main image of the building interior will need to be duplicated twice and portions cut away. The trapeze artists are in a single image, but you need to separate them so they can move independently. In order to do this, the fingers of the woman will have to be redrawn slightly, but they don't have to be perfect because the image will never be static.

Once the images have been assembled (in Photoshop), they have to be exported in a Web format that recognizes transparency so the images, but not the backgrounds, can be imported into Flash. This means that you have the choice of GIF or PNG. Our example uses GIF, and each image is optimized to the bare minimum of colours (for these images that means tones of grey). The main background is the building.gif image, which has been reduced to just four colours – the inevitable pixelation is a visual bonus. To achieve the candle glow, the entire scene has to be darkened.

❶

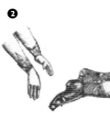

❷

TIP

Putting things into perspective

When using 'found' images, try and identify visual opportunities. For example, this background image has a vanishing point drawn in, so use this as the start point for the woman in the green dress. Notice how she pauses at the threshold before altering direction as she 'enters' the building.

❸

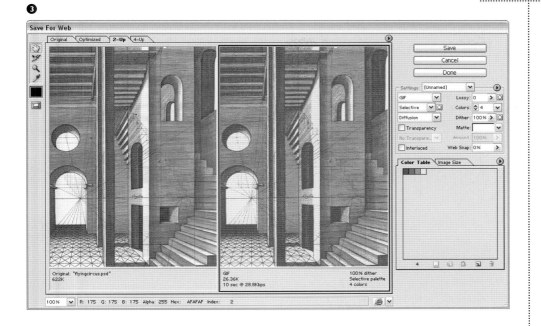

❹

❶ The first task is to assemble the master images in Photoshop. The size of the animation is 340 x 468 pixels, so the building interior will have to be this size. To accommodate the oversized lady image, the master image document will have to be larger. Use 980 x 750 pixels, so that other visual elements can be displayed. The resolution should be 72 dpi. Duplicate the building and cut parts away so that a figure can appear in the window opening and travel behind the post.

❷ The detail shows the retouching that should be done to separate the woman's hands from the man's feet.

❸ Each of the nine elements should be exported individually in GIF format, so start with the building interior. Go to *File > Save for Web* and the ImageReady Export panel will appear. Select GIF as the export format and reduce the colours from 256 to just four. Set *Diffusion* and *Dither* to 100 per cent. The reduction to four colours – actually greys – combined with the diffusion and dither will create an interesting texture while keeping the file size to a minimum. Export the two building details at the same specification.

❹ Now export the lady image. Select GIF as the export format and reduce the colours from 256 to 16, making *Diffusion* and *Dither* 100 per cent, but also select *Transparency* this time. Continue exporting the remaining elements to this new specification, but reduce their colours to eight.

5 Now move to Flash and start to create the animation. In *Movie Properties*, change the size to 340 x 468 pixels. This is a complex 12-layer animation, so it is helpful to fast forwards here and take a look at the timeline of the completed animation. You will see the familiar visual elements (which you exported as GIFs) in separate layers. There are other elements essential to the animation, but these will be described as and when necessary. The completed timeline will appear in all the following screenshots so that you can refer to it.

6 Each visual element has to be imported into Flash, so go to *Library* > '+' > **Symbol** and name this new symbol 'Building'. Repeat the process with all other imported elements. Create a new layer for each of them in the order shown on the timeline (ignoring any layers that you have not yet created material for).

7 The *Library* panel will now look like this.

8 At frame 1 on the Building Interior layer, go to the Library and drag an instance of the Building symbol on stage. Use *Effects* > **Tint Colour** (or *Colour* > **Tint** from the *Properties* window in Flash MX) to apply a yellow tint to the image.

9 At frames 27 and 42 add keyframes. At 42, using the *Transform* panel, increase the scaling to 200 per cent and position the image so that the window is central in the frame. Then go to *Frame* > **Motion Tweening**, or *Tween* > **Motion** in Flash MX, to add tweening with its default values.

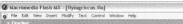

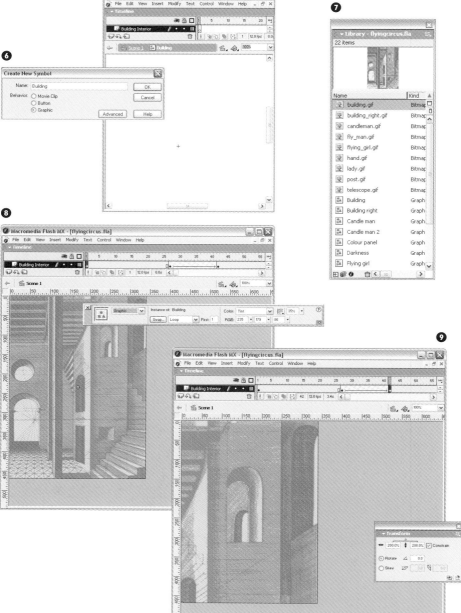

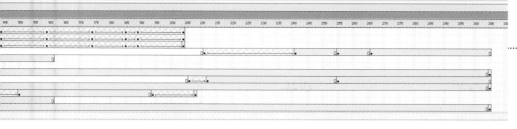

⓾

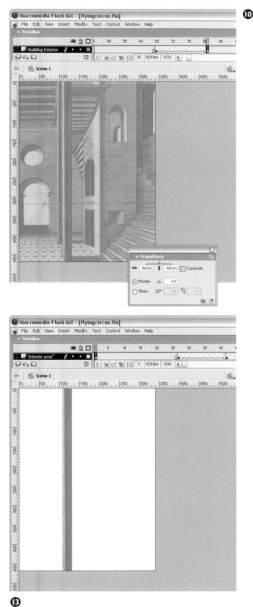

⓰

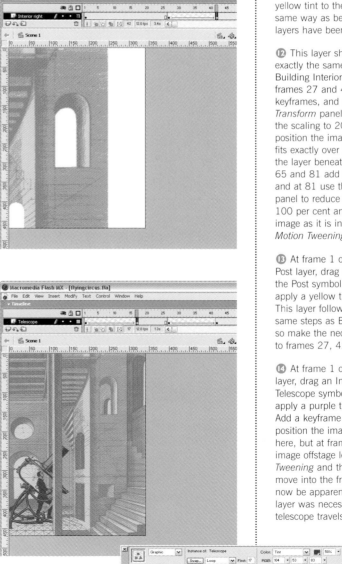

⓭

⓮

⓾ At frames 65 and 81 add keyframes. At 81 use the *Transform* panel to reduce the scaling to 100 per cent and position the image as it is in frame 1. Add *Motion Tweening* with default values selected.

At frame 1 on the Interior Right layer, drag an Instance of the Building Right symbol onstage. Use *Tint Colour* to apply a yellow tint to the image in the same way as before. The other layers have been hidden.

⓰ This layer should follow exactly the same steps as the Building Interior layer. So at frames 27 and 42 add keyframes, and at 42 use the *Transform* panel to increase the scaling to 200 per cent and position the image so that it fits exactly over the image on the layer beneath. At frames 65 and 81 add keyframes, and at 81 use the *Transform* panel to reduce the scaling to 100 per cent and position the image as it is in frame 1. Add *Motion Tweening*.

⓭ At frame 1 on the Interior Post layer, drag an instance of the Post symbol on stage and apply a yellow tint to the image. This layer follows exactly the same steps as Building Interior so make the necessary changes to frames 27, 42, 65 and 81.

⓮ At frame 1 on the Telescope layer, drag an Instance of the Telescope symbol onstage and apply a purple tint to the image. Add a keyframe at frame 17, position the image as shown here, but at frame 1 drag the image offstage left. Add *Motion Tweening* and the telescope will move into the frame. It should now be apparent why the Post layer was necessary, as the telescope travels behind it.

104

⑮ This layer should follow exactly the same steps as before, so make the necessary changes at frames 27, 42, 65 and 81. The screenshot shows the telescope in mid tween.

⑯ At frame 42 on the Hand layer, drag an instance of the Hand on stage and apply a blue tint to it. Place another keyframe at frame 55 and add *Motion Tweening*.

⑰ Return to frame 42 and drag the hand offstage right. The *Onion Skin* view shows how the tween moves the hand into the frame. Add keyframes at frames 65 and 81 and reverse the process so the hand moves out again.

This is a good point to recap on what you have achieved so far in the animation. The telescope moves into frame pointing at the window in the top right, you then zoom into that window and see a pointing hand emerge 'through' the window.

⑱ At frame 92 on the Lady layer, go to the *Library* panel to drag an Instance of the lady onstage and then select *Effects > Advanced* to apply a green tint to the image. Notice the Alpha transparency is 80 per cent. Use the *Transform* panel to rescale her to 13 per cent so she fits in the doorway.

⑲ Drag the keyframe back to frame 82 and add another keyframe at 92. At frame 82 go to *Effects > Advanced > Alpha Transparency*, or *Colour > Advanced* in Flash MX. Set *Alpha* to 0 per cent. Use the *Transform* window to rescale the lady and position her on the vanishing point of the lines on the Building Interior layer. Now add *Motion Tweening* with its default settings.

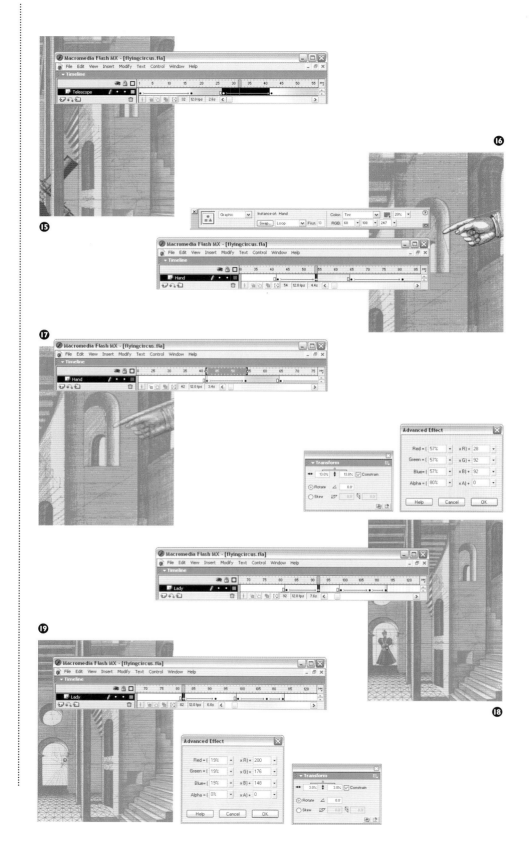

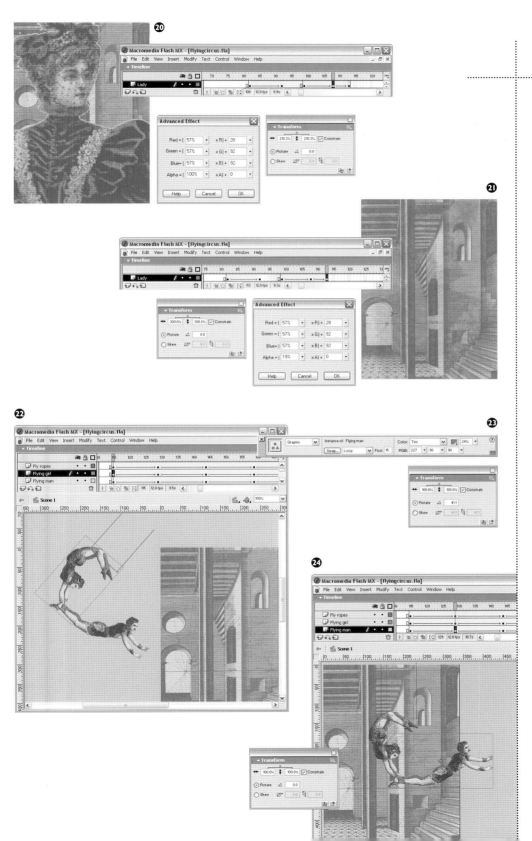

20 Add keyframes at frame 99, 108 and 113. At 108 increase the Alpha transparency to 100 per cent. Use the *Transform* panel to rescale her to about 210 per cent and position her as here.

21 At frame 113 reduce the Alpha transparency to 19 per cent. Use the *Transform* panel to rescale her to about 300 per cent and position her as here. Add *Motion Tweening*.

22 Now work on the trapeze artists. They appear to pivot from a point offstage, make two passes back and forth across the stage and, on the second pass, the girl releases her grip and the man flies off. This view is zoomed to 70 per cent to show the work area outside the animation frame.

23 The keen-eyed among you will notice that ropes have appeared from nowhere on the example. We will return to them presently, but first, at frame 115 on the Flying Girl and Flying Man layers, drag the relevant Instances onstage and use the *Effects > Tint Colour*, or *Colour > Tint* in Flash MX, to apply a red tint to the images. Position both images offstage to the left and rotate them by about 41°.

24 At frame 129 add a keyframe to both the Flying Girl and Flying Man layers and position them so that the trampoline is hanging vertically (0° rotation) in the centre of the frame.

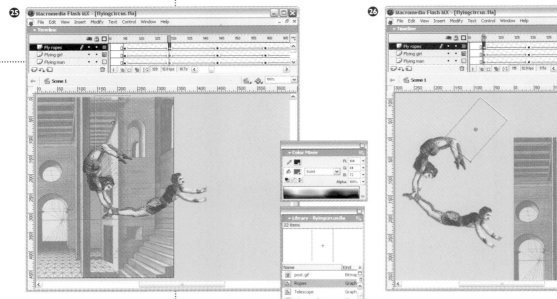

25 Now add a layer called 'Fly Ropes'. Add a keyframe at frame 129 and set *Stroke* to 1 pixel and *Colour* to RGB 104/84/72 and use the Pencil tool to draw the two ropes. Use *Insert > Convert to Symbol* and name the image 'Ropes'.

26 Drag this keyframe back to frame 115 and create a new keyframe to replace it at frame 129. At frame 115 drag the instance offstage left and rotate it so that it 'connects' with the trapeze bar.

27 Add keyframes to these three layers at frames 144, 159 and 174 and position the three images in the 'swing' positions.

28 Add keyframes to these three layers at frames 185 and, on the Flying Man layer, move the image slightly away from the girl's hand, so that she loses her grip on his ankles.

29 Add keyframes to these three layers, and then at frames 189 on the Flying Girl and Ropes layers, position the images vertically. On the Flying Man layer, move the image further to the right, partially offstage.

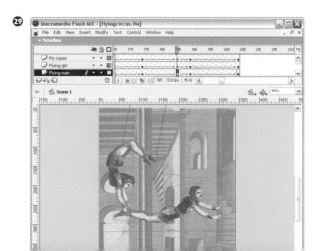

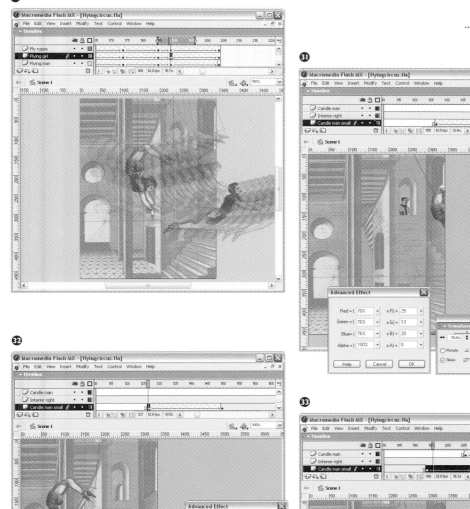

30 To complete the trapeze part add keyframes to these three layers at frame 204, and move the images so the girl completes her second swing while the man flies completely offstage. The partial *Onion Skin* view will show this more clearly. Add *Frame > Motion Tweening*, or *Tween > Motion* from the *Properties* window in Flash MX, between all the keyframes created for the trapeze artists.

31 You have already created a 'Candle Man' layer in step six. Now create another named 'Candle Man Small' below the Interior right layer (it must be beneath, so the man can appear at the window). At frame 150 drag an Instance of the Candle man symbol onstage and use *Effects > Advanced* to apply a purple tint to the image. Use the *Transform* panel to reduce his size to 70 per cent.

32 Drag this keyframe back to frame 127 and add another to replace it at frame 150. At frame 127 drag the image towards the bottom left so that none of it appears at the window. Set *Effects > Advanced > Alpha Transparency* to 0 per cent. The size should remain the same at 70 per cent. Add *Motion Tweening*.

33 At frames 194 and 208 add new keyframes. At frame 194 the man is obscured by the woman swinging in front of him so the screenshot is taken at frame 196.

108

34 At frame 208 go to
*Effects > Advanced > Alpha
Transparency*, or *Colour >
Advanced* in Flash MX, and
change it to 18 per cent. Then
add *Motion Tweening*. You will
notice that a ghosted image of
a larger man has appeared.

35 At frame 212 on the Candle
Man layer, drag an instance of
the Candle Man onstage and
use *Effects > Advanced* (or
Colour > Advanced) to apply
the same purple tint to the
image as you did in step 31.
The Alpha transparency should
be at 100 per cent and the
scaling at the default of 100
per cent.

36 Drag the keyframe back to
frame 206 and add another
at frame 212 to replace it. At
frame 206 reduce the Alpha
transparency to 0 per cent and
add *Motion Tweening*. Now
recap what you have achieved
since step 18. The lady has
appeared in the distance,
paused at the doorway, moved
towards the viewer, then faded.
The trapeze artistes have swung
across the stage twice; on the
second occasion the flying girl
lost her grip on the flying man.
The candle man has emerged
from the window at the top of
the stairs, faded, then re-
emerged at the foot.

37 In the latter part of the
animation, the man shifts his
head forwards, appearing to
blow out the candle, and the
scene fades to darkness. You
need another version of the
candle man, so copy the image,
go to *Library > '+' > Symbol*
and call this 'Candle Man 2',
pasting in the image. Use the
Lasso to define two areas, one
around the head, the other
around the flame. Rotate both
slightly anti-clockwise and then
Group the image.

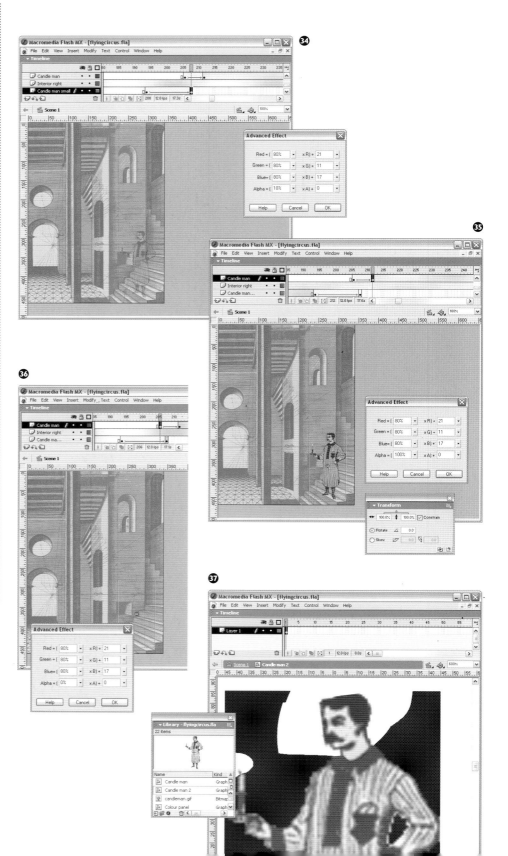

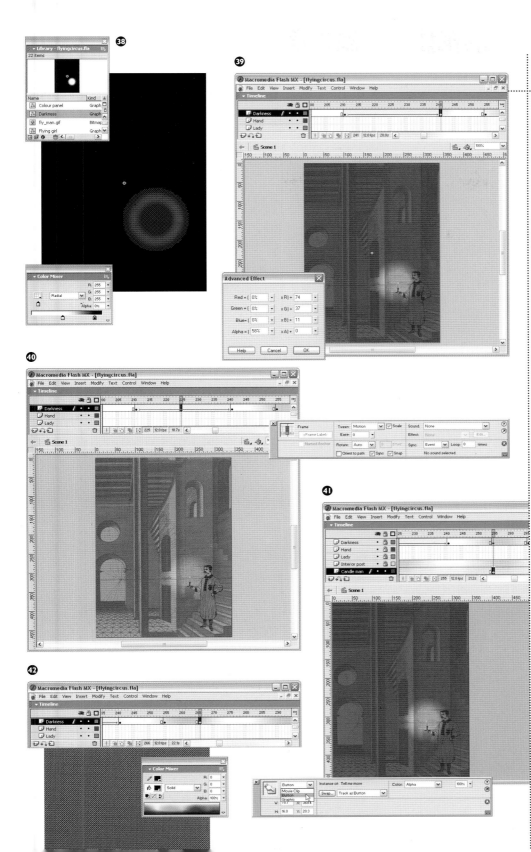

38 Create a new symbol named 'Darkness' and then, using the *Rectangle* tool, with *Stroke* set to *Nil* and *Fill* set to black, draw a rectangle sized 340 x 468 pixels covering the entire stage. Draw a circle towards the bottom right, having kept the *Stroke* at *Nil* but using the *Fill* panel with a *Radial Gradient* of white to black. Using the *Mixer* panel, set the Alpha transparency value to 0 per cent. Use the sliders on the Fill panel to refine the shape.

39 Create a new layer named 'Darkness' and add a keyframe at frame 241. Drag an Instance of the darkness symbol on stage and go to *Effects* > *Advanced* or *Colour* > *Advanced* in MX and make it 58 per cent.

40 Click in the timeline between these two frames and add *Motion Tweening*. The screenshot shows a midway position: the darkness appears with a 'hole' left for the glow.

41 In the Candle Man layer at frame 255, add a blank keyframe. Drag an Instance of Candle Man 2 onstage.

42 Now return to the Darkness layer. At frame 266 add a blank keyframe. Use the *Rectangle* tool with *Stroke* set to *Nil* and *Fill* set to RGB 104/84/72. Draw a rectangle sized 340 x 468 pixels to cover the entire stage. Since step 36, a duplicate candle man has been created with the head thrust slightly forwards, appearing to blow out the candle, plus a layer that contains the darkness with the candle glow cutout. A few frames after this, Candle Man 2 appears to blow out the candle and the animation ends with a darkened screen. This should finish on frame 305.

110 CLOWNING AROUND

This is an animation without movement! In actual fact, the user provides the motion using the mouse. DHTML animation uses layers fixed to a timeline, but you can also forget about the timeline and let the user drag the layers (which contain images) to their preferred location.

The first task is to find or create the images. If you scan them (as we did here from a copyright-free resource), all the images except the background face have to be cut out, so they have a transparent background. This is easily done using a bitmap application like Photoshop.

Convert them to GIF format at the lowest possible colour depth to keep the file size small. Fortunately this type of image is tolerant of low-quality settings. Using draggable layers is a simple and much underused technique on the Web. However, if you want to convert this to a conventional animation, then add a timeline, place each layer on it and simply record the movement of an image from the border to a position on top of the empty clown face.

TIP

Cartoon strip

This idea has many applications. You could swap the heads and the bodies on your vacation photographs, drag your head onto a famous body, or even peel off the clothes on a virtual strippergram!

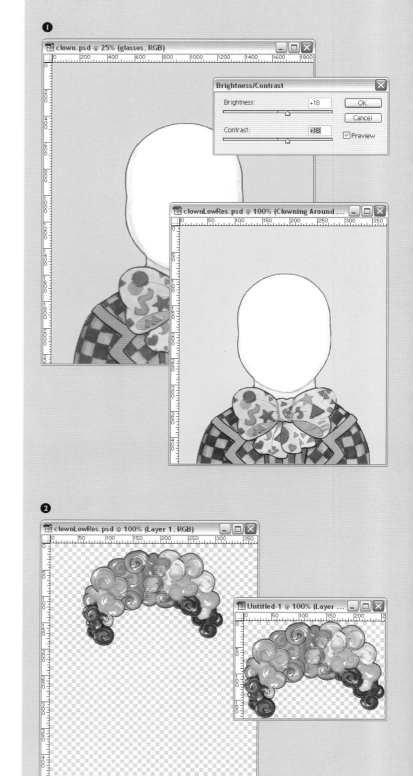

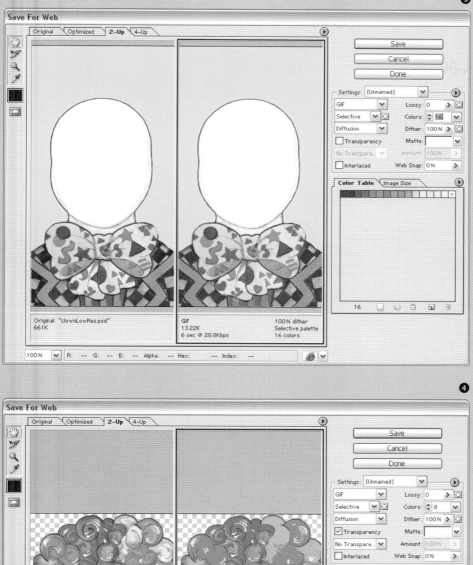

❸

❹

❶ Create the images either onscreen or by scanning the original art into a bitmap application. We scanned at 400 dpi and assembled the images in a single-layered Photoshop file. The image should be reduced to the desired size, 376 x 450 pixels, and the resolution changed to 72 dpi. The layered file means all the images will be changed together. The clown images need to be bright and full of contrast – use your application's *Image Adjust* > **Brightness and Contrast** control set at level 18 to achieve this. This correction will help when exporting the images as GIFs. File sizes will be smaller if you reduce the number of colours that each GIF uses to display the image.

❷ Once you are satisfied with your collection of images, start exporting each in GIF format. If you are using Photoshop, turn off all but the desired layer and make sure that, if you have a white background layer, this too is turned off. Copy each layer and *Paste* into a new document with *Contents* set to *Transparent*. This reduces the canvas size to that of the individual image.

❸ Use Save for the Web and select GIF. Then choose Selective, and reduce the number of colours to the minimum. You can also try selecting *Dither* and *Diffusion* to see if these improve the image quality. Images of a related type will usually accept a similar colour reduction. The clown images in the example have been optimized to between 6 and 16 colours.

❹ Check that the *Transparency* tick box is selected for all but the background image. Click *OK*.

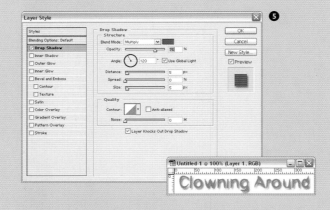

112

⑤ Create the title in a suitable font – try Chocolate Bandit – and select Layer Effect to add a purple drop shadow to the title. Export this as a GIF too. This image will be static on the webpage, so it does not need a transparent background. A white background will also result in a smooth drop shadow.

⑥ The image preparation is complete, so now go to Dreamweaver (or your preferred application) to create the animation. The main clown image size is 376 x 450 pixels in size, and should be placed within a layer named 'Clown' that is positioned *L* (left) 286 pixels and *T* (top) 93 pixels. This size and position results in the image being more or less centred within the width of a browser window, maximized within the target monitor resolution of 1024 x 768 pixels.

⑦ Add another layer above and import the title image. Add the text subhead as default (HTML) text.

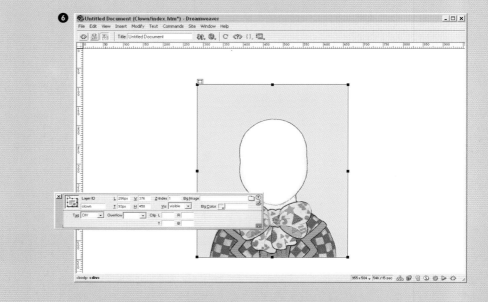

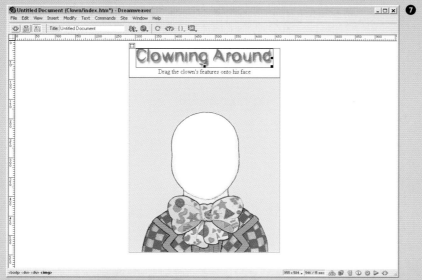

❽

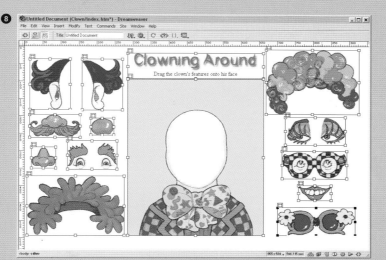

❽ Create the remaining layers and place a single image within each. (Layer names will be used by the JavaScript that Dreamweaver creates automatically, and so must not include spaces. They can *contain* numerals, but should not *begin* with one.)

❾ Select the *Body Tag* at the far left of the Dreamweaver screen, then select one of the layers to be dragged – HairLeft for example. Then go to *Behaviors > Drag Layer*. Select the HairLeft layer from this menu and accept the default settings. The *Bring Layer to Front* option is important, and the default *Leave on Top* option means that as each layer is moved this one stays on top of the others.

❿ Test your page in Microsoft's Internet Explorer browser because it will not function properly in all versions of Netscape. Drag the images into position; clicking on any one will bring it to the front of the stacking order.

❾

❿

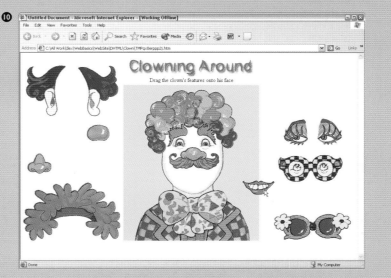

114 TOY BOX

This Flash-based project started life as an image from a silhouette source book. Imagine making a simple cut-out paper puppet with the limbs jointed with pins or thread and you will see the idea. The original artwork has got to be scanned first. CorelTrace is a good application to do this in because the image can then be scanned, traced and converted to vector format. To enable the limbs and head to be animated, it has to be broken up into its constituent parts. CorelDraw's *Trim* tool is an easy way to crudely chop up, the image. Once the parts are cleaned up, the entire image can be saved and exported in a suitable vector format like AI or EPS. (Flash does not currently have a Corel import filter.) Then you can assemble the animation with Flash. The body, head and four limbs are separated, converted to symbols and placed on six separate layers. By adding a keyframe and repositioning the parts, you create the animation. Always remember that the head and limbs 'connect' to the body with imaginary joints. Once these six layers are animated, you can add the strings on a new layer. The finishing touches are the addition of a shadow, a changing background colour and an oval surround in the foreground. Finally the animation is placed in a webpage with a heading, a line of text and a tiled background image.

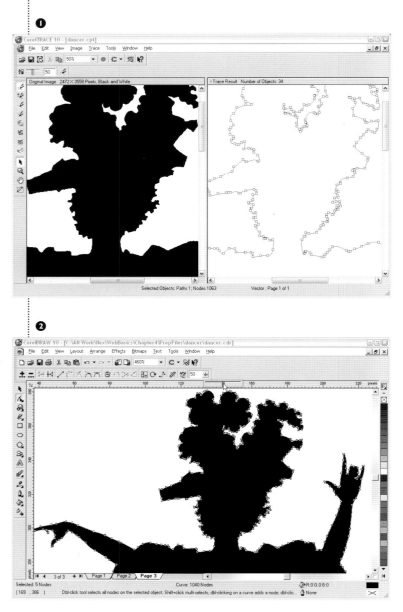

❶

❷

TIP

Puppetmaster

In order for the head and limbs to appear to pivot around those imaginary joints, you may wish to create a small circle on each part as a guide. As long as these are on the symbols before you add keyframes, they will appear on each image. When you are happy with the animation, simply remove the white circles from each symbol and they will disappear.

1 After the scan is complete, select *Outline Trace* and change the *Accuracy* setting to 50 per cent to reduce the complexity of the outline.

2 Depending on the application you used, either export the traced image in a suitable vector format or simply paste it directly into a new CorelDraw document. Rescale the image to fit within an area 300 x 400 pixels (the size of the animation). In fact, it is best to change your page setup to this size as well. The image is selected using the *Curve* tool; this shows the number of nodes (or anchor points) that the original contains. Use the *Curve Smoothness* slider to smooth out the shape – 50 per cent is a suitable amount for this shape. Always reduce the complexity of vector images converted from bitmaps as much as possible; very complex shapes will put more demands on a computer and reduce some of the advantages that a vector image has over a bitmap.

3 Duplicate the image and drag the original aside. Using the *Trim* tool, roughly separate all the elements. Keep duplicating and trimming until you have a body, a head and neck, and four limbs. This has been shown here in Corel *Wireframe* mode.

4 Use the *Shape* tool to clean up and extend the shapes so that they can overlap the body. Ensure that the open ends of the shapes are joined, otherwise they will not refill with black.

5 The final shapes should look like this. Select the image and export in AI format, using default settings.

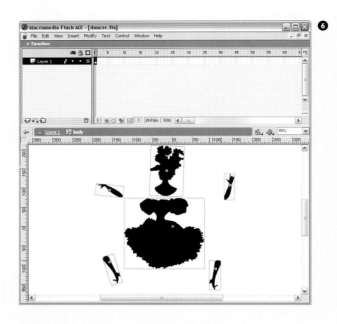

116

6 Once in the Flash domain, each part of the image must be converted to a symbol. Go to *Library* > '+' to create a new symbol called 'Body'.

7 Individually select the head and each limb, then cut them so that only the body remains. Create a new symbol for each element and paste in the relevant part of the body. The elements are now stored in the *Library* and ready to use.

8 From the *Library* panel drag an Instance of each symbol onstage into a new layer. The timeline will now look like this.

9 To create the animation, add a keyframe after five frames in each layer and adjust the position of the parts, so that they move like a marionette supported by strings. Add *Frame* > **Motion Tweening**, or *Tween* > **Motion** from the *Properties* window in Flash MX, with the default settings between each keyframe. Keep testing the overall image as you do this to see that it moves convincingly.

10 Repeat this process until you have added about 12 sets of keyframes. The animation will loop, so the first and last frames must be in similar positions – otherwise a jerky step will be noticeable.

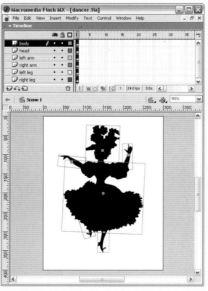

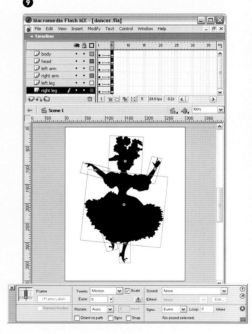

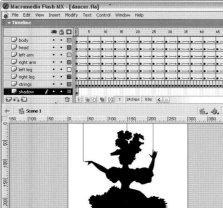

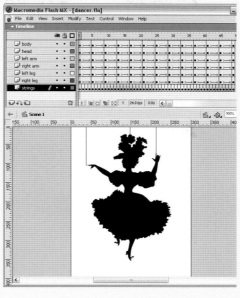

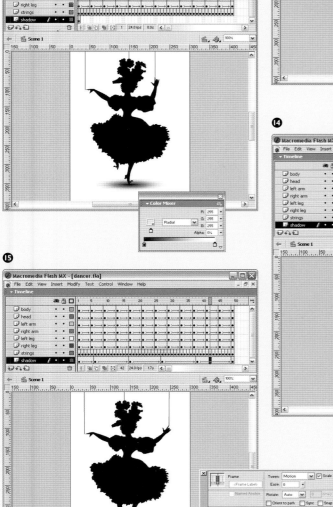

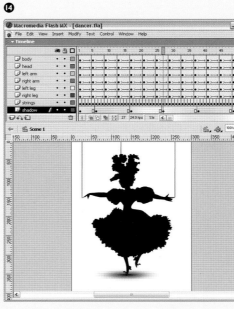

⓫ Use *Movie Properties* to adjust the *Frame Rate* until you are happy with the result.

⓬ Now add a new layer for the three strings and draw them in, using *Hairline* as the stroke thickness. Keep adding keyframes and repositioning, shortening or lengthening the lines to connect them to the hair and hands. Unfortunately, this task has to be done manually on a frame-by-frame basis, because Tweening will not work on objects that have to be ungrouped and altered at each keyframe.

⓭ Now add a new layer for the shadow. Use an ellipse, with *Stroke* set to *Nil* and a *Radial Fill* of black to white with the white set to Alpha 0 per cent. Draw a flattened oval shape. Then go to *Insert > **Convert to Symbol***, call it 'Shadow', and set its *Behavior* to *Graphic*.

⓮ Add additional keyframes at each point where the feet or foot touches the ground, and move the shadow so that it is centred beneath them.

⓯ Add in *Motion Tweening* with its default values.

118

16 Add another new layer for the background – draw a rectangle 300 x 400 pixels with *Stroke* set to *Nil* and a *Gradient Fill* of black to white. Convert this to a symbol graphic and name it 'Background'.

17 Go to *Frame > Effects > Advanced*, or *Colour > Advanced* in Flash MX, and use the sliders to create colour in the background.

18 Add a keyframe at roughly the halfway point and use the *Advanced* sliders again to create a different colour in the background.

19 Add a keyframe at the last frame and set the colour to the same as it is in frame 1. Add *Motion Tweening* to this and the background will change gradually as the tween progresses.

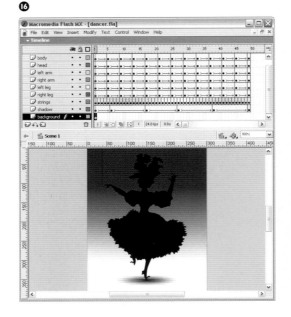

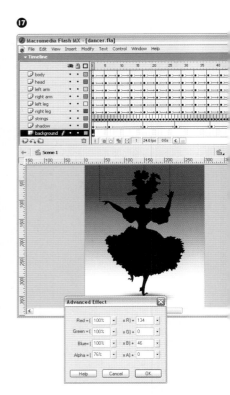

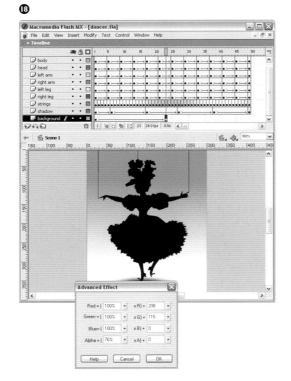

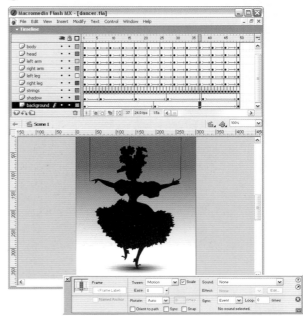

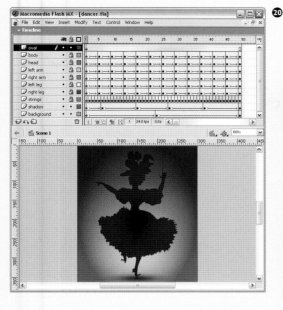

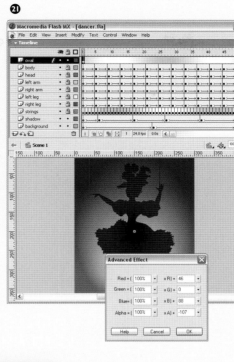

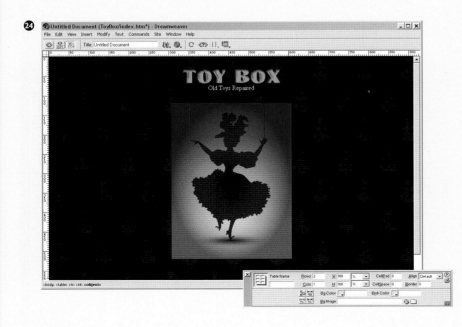

20 Finally, create the foreground oval that frames the animation. Draw a rectangle 300 x 400 pixels in size with *Stroke* set to *Nil* and a *Radial Fill* of black to white. Use *Insert > Convert to Symbol* and name the new symbol 'Oval'.

21 Using a symbol, even if an image is not being tweened, enables the *Effects > Advanced* menu sliders, or *Colour > Advanced* in Flash MX, to be employed for the colour. Add frames to this layer to complete the animation, which can now be exported.

22 The animation is placed in an HTML page above a tiled background that repeats the dancer image. To create this image, import the original dancer file, reduce it to a convenient size, then duplicate it and position the second image diagonally offset from the first. Now *Merge Visible* the two dancers. Export this finished image as a GIF, optimized to four colours.

23 Create the heading in a suitable font and apply *Layer Effects > Inner Shadow*. Add a black background panel underneath and export this image as a GIF too, optimized to 16 colours.

24 Switch to an HTML application, such as Dreamweaver, and on a new blank page create a table 100 per cent x 100 per cent with two rows. Place the heading followed by a line of HTML text in the top row and the Flash image in the bottom, ensuring that *Center* and *Middle* are selected for the image positions within the cells.

120 SOMETHING FISHY

You may have come to the conclusion that Flash is the only way to create really sophisticated Web animations, but DHTML can also produce some great results. It is used here along with Dreamweaver, which is where the animation is assembled. To enable the fishes to have natural-looking movement, their progress back and forth is plotted on paths controlled by keyframes. To allow the fish to swim 'behind' some of the weed, you will have to create these as separate images and place them on layers above the fish. The other two weeds are painted onto the background tank image.

This tank is saved as a JPEG image while the fish and weed are all in transparent GIF format. You will need two images for each fish – one facing left and the other right – because Dreamweaver DHTML doesn't have a *Flip* command. When you attempt a 'natural' animation, observation of the real thing is very important. Here the shoal of fish swims quickly and closely together, the orange guppy moves in an undulating, more sedate manner while the loach skulks around the bottom. At 117KB the combined file size is quite large – the HTML page (index.htm) alone is 61KB, because it contains all the animation instructions.

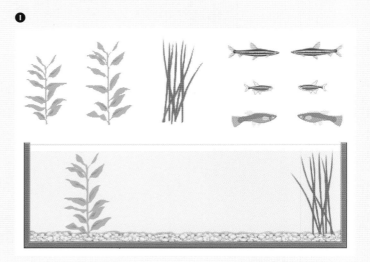

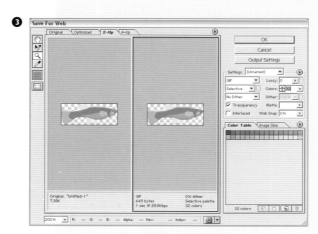

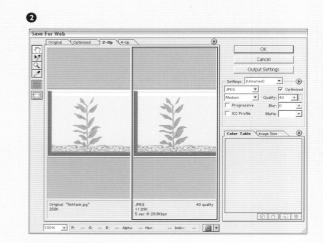

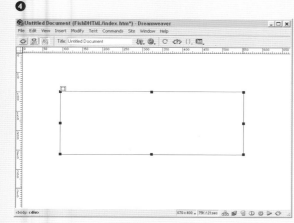

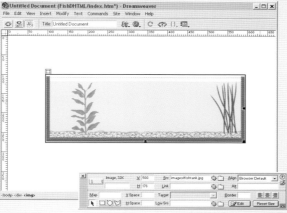

1 Create the images by scanning original art, or use a bitmap application like Photoshop to draw them from scratch. Before starting any work, make a few sketches to plan how the pieces of your animation will look and develop. You will need both left- and right-facing fish, as well as some duplicate weed!

2 Each element must be saved as a separate image file, so start with the tank. Select *File > Save for Web > JPG/JPEG*, then optimize it to the lowest acceptable quality level. In this example it is 40.

3 Next, create the Fish and Weed images on a transparent background. Use the same process as before to save them, but this time select the *Transparent GIF* format, optimizing to reduce the colours to the minimum acceptable number. In this example it's 32.

4 In Dreamweaver, or another HTML editing application, start to assemble the animation on a blank page of about 670 x 400 pixels in size. Draw the first layer, which is for the tank.

5 Make sure the *Prevent Overlaps* box is not selected within the *Layer Properties* dialog box, and then insert your background tank image.

6 Create additional layers above this and place a fish image into each one. There are both left- and right-facing, fish and the small, shoal fish needs two additional pairs layered in to make the shoal. (The order can be rearranged later if necessary.)

122

❼ Finally, add two layers above the others and insert the two weed images. As you will see, the fish will swim above the background tank image but behind the two weed images.

❽ At this stage it is very important to give each of the layers a name, to avoid any confusion once the animation becomes more complex. In this instance the names should be specific to the fish type and the direction they move in.

❾ Open *Window > **Timeline***. Select the first layer to add to the animation, in this case the fish at the bottom called 'LoachR'. Now select *Modify > Timeline > **Add Object to Timeline***.

❿ Select the last frame in the timeline and drag it to frame 120. At this stage the exact duration and speed of the fish movement is at the 'experimental' stage and can be modified later if required.

❽

Name	Z
WeedL	15
WeedR	14
LoachR	14
LoachL	13
GuppieR	12
GuppieL	11
Tetra1L	9
Tetra1R	8
Tetra2L	7
Tetra2R	6
Tetra3L	5
Tetra3R	4
Tetra4L	3
Tetra4R	2
Background	1

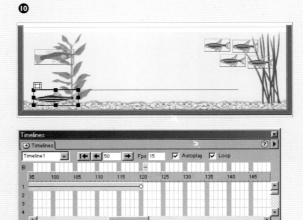

⓫

⓬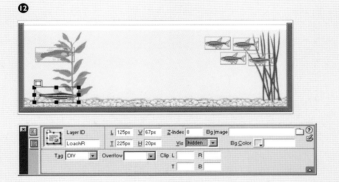

⓭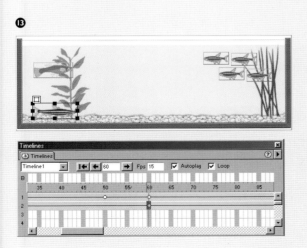

⓫ Select frame 50 and click *Timeline Arrow* > **Add Keyframe**. This frame is for positioning the layer on the left. Now drag the layer to the desired position on the left of the fish tank. The animation guideline will now appear.

⓬ The next stage is to introduce the layer that will hold the image which swims in the other direction (LoachR). To position this layer on the page, you need the coordinates of the first layer (LoachL) at frame 50. Open the *Properties* panel and make a note of the *L* (left) and *T* (top) positions of the layer; apply them to frame 1 of the new layer (LoachR). Next, add this layer to the timeline using the same method as in step nine. Now that you have the two layers sitting on top of each other, it is necessary to hide the second layer (LoachR) until it is required for the movement back to the other side. To do this, select frame 1 on *Timeline2* and select *Properties* > *Vis (visibility options)* > **Hidden**.

⓭ Add another keyframe at frame 60 on both *Timeline1* and 2. This will be the point at which the LoachR layer starts to move to the right, and the LoachL layer becomes hidden. This ensures that the change of image is as seamless as possible. The position of the first frame, LoachL, remains the same for frames 50 and 60, which creates a slight delay before it starts to move again. Select frame 60 on *Timeline1* and apply a *Hidden* visibility state, then apply a *Visible* state to *Timeline2*.

124

⓮ Next position the LoachR layer on the right. Make a note of the left and top pixel position of frame 120 on *Timeline1*, then apply it to the same frame on *Timeline2*. Add a keyframe on frame 110 of *Timeline2*, which once again halts the layer and creates a slight delay before they swap. You also need to change the visibility of both layers; apply a *Hidden* state to *Timeline2* at frame 120, and a *Visible* state to *Timeline1*. At this stage you should assess the animation. Select *Autoplay* and *Loop* on the *Properties* panel, then press *F12* to open the browser window. You should now be able to see the simple movement of the fish moving from left to right.

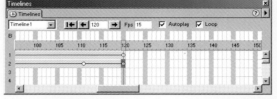

⓯ The next stage is to add keyframes on the timelines. By adding keyframes along a timeline, you can then drag the layer to a desired position. This part of the process is completely random; you can apply and move the frames wherever it looks appropriate, and add as many frames as you like. In this instance we have added two at frames 15 and 35, and moved the layers only slightly off the horizontal, because the fish is moving along the bottom of the tank.

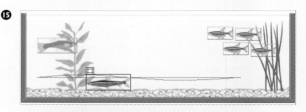

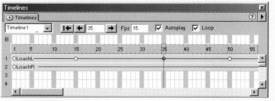

⓰ Now you have the complete loop for the fish moving from one side of the tank to the other, so this principle can be applied to each of the layers in turn. Work on one fish at a time, using the same process. Gradually apply all the frames and their visibility states and remember to preview the work in your browser regularly to see the animation developing. Remember, you can drag the keyframes to any position to create the effect you want.

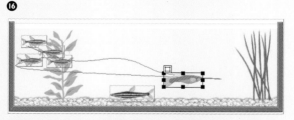

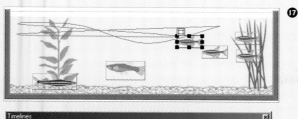

17 To avoid the layers all moving at the same speed and direction at the same time, it is necessary to add more frames to some of the layers. The group of four shoal fish move from one side to the other twice while the other fish only loop once. By adding two extra sets of keyframes on the left, and then on the right, you can add more speed to the fish. The first set of frames to move to the left are at frame 25, while on frame 65 the set should be moved to the right. Add additional keyframes at frame 87 on the timelines to move them back to the left, and on the final frame, 120, move the layers back to the right. With the fish that are moving faster, there will not be any time delay between the switching between *Hidden* and *Visible* states.

18 Once all the animation positioning has been finalized through constant testing and moving to achieve the desired effect, all that remains is to add the final layers containing the water plants. Add these above the fish, so that they swim behind. This will add depth to your animation.

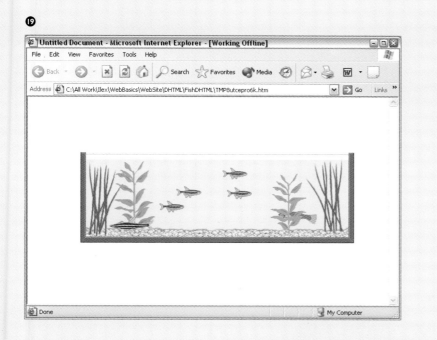

19 Your completed animation is now ready for viewing in your browser.

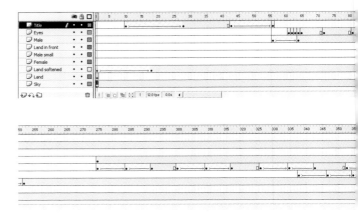

126 ASCENT OF MAN

This Flash animation lasts for 42 seconds, contains over 500 frames and weighs in at only 25kb. In order for you to get an idea of the whole animation, the timeline is shown in its entirety (*above right*). There are periods of inactivity in each layer, which are shown as blank frames on the timeline. This is because timing is as important as images.

This animation is a story without words, so it is important to plan the narrative before starting the animation. As you can see, after creating the background, the Land layer containing the three hills is duplicated. The original will not be used again, but is best retained in case you decide to make changes later. This new 'Land Softened' layer is modified using the *Soften Edges Modifier*. The soft edge is, in fact, a series of borders, each increasing in transparency. The three hills are drawn oversized so that only the 'soft' edge at the top is visible.

This animation again makes frequent use of the *Motion Tweening* technique of *Easing*. When the characters 'bounce', they decelerate towards the top and accelerate towards the bottom as they fall (see our Tip below). The male and female characters can be drawn in your favourite vector application and imported, or drawn directly in Flash (ensure that any unnecessary anchor points are removed and then convert them to symbols). Although their movement is controlled using *Motion Tweening*, the eyes are placed on a different layer so that they can be repositioned for each keyframe.

The importance of story

Make sure that you have a clear storyline before starting a character animation, even though you may decide to amend it part way through. The concept for this animation is the world's oldest story, Adam and Eve, or boy meets girl. The male character is happily bouncing through life when he suddenly becomes aware of a female. He peeps out of his crater and so does she, but withdraws at first. He immediately follows. She emerges first from the centre crater with him following on behind. The background dissolves with the happy couple emerging full screen.

❶

❷

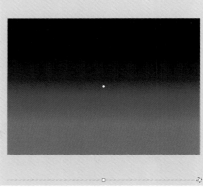

T I P

Tween age rebellion

To begin the motion, tween slowly and accelerate the tween towards the end of the animation. Drag the slider up or enter a value between −1 and −100. To begin the motion, to tween rapidly, and decelerate it towards the end of the animation, drag the slider down or enter a positive value between 1 and 100.

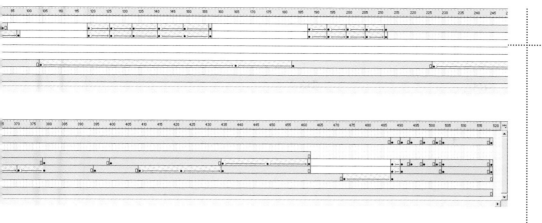

❶ Using the default movie size, create a new background and call it 'Sky'. Then set *Stroke* to *Nil* and *Fill* to *Linear Gradient* using R102/G102/B255, drawing a rectangle of 550 x 400 pixels.

❷ Use the *Fill Transform* tool to rotate the fill so that it runs top to bottom. Turn off the visibility for this layer.

❸ On a new layer called Land, use *Pencil* > **Ink** mode to draw an outline for the three hills. This outline must be drawn oversize to allow an excess of about 20 pixels at the sides and bottom, so ensure that *View* > **Work Area** is selected in order for you to use the area outside the visible stage.

❹ Fill this shape using the current *Fill* and *Transform Fill* settings.

❺ Remove the *Stroke* (outline) from the image.

❻ Using the *Subselect* tool, adjust the anchor points until you are satisfied with the shape.

❼ With the settings unchanged, draw the three craters, deleting the Stroke (outline). Do not use *Transform Fill* this time; you want a linear blend running left to right.

❽ Go to *Insert* > **Convert to Symbol**, naming it 'Land'. Then select *Behavior* > **Graphic**. Once saved as a symbol, the Land layer plays no further part in the animation. (It is often easier to create images onstage rather than directly in the *Library* because the stage area is not visible in the *Library* environment.)

❸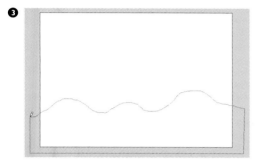

❹

❺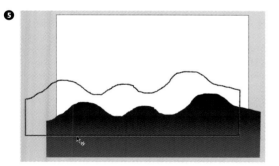

❻

❼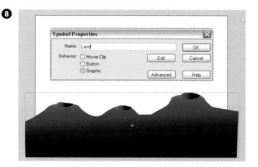

❽

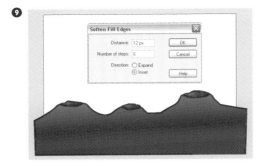

9 Create a new layer called 'Land Softened' and drag an Instance of the Land symbol into it. Select *Modify > Shape > **Soften Fill Edges*** and change the settings to 12 pixels, 6 steps, inset.

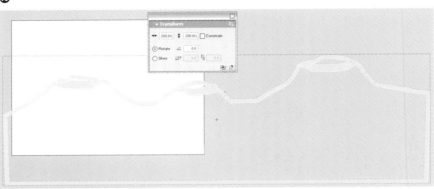

10 At keyframe 1, which was automatically created when you dragged the Land Instance onstage, use the *Transform* panel to scale the image to 200 per cent and drag it stage right. This is best shown in *Outline View* for clarity.

11 Convert this image to a new symbol named 'Land Softened' and then add another keyframe at frame 18.

12 Return to frame 1 and go to *Effects > **Alpha Transparency***, or *Colour > **Alpha*** in Flash MX, to set it at 0 per cent.

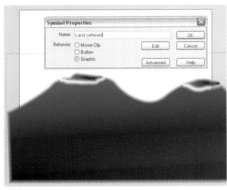

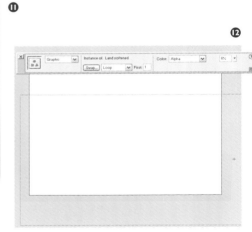

13 Return to frame 18 and this time increase Alpha transparency to 32 per cent. With the visibility of the Sky layer restored, the animation looks like this.

14 Now move onto the characters. Both male and female have been predrawn in the example within Illustrator and are imported into Flash as black shapes. Click on *Library > + > **Symbol***, name it 'Male' and import the image.

15 Pick a *Radial Gradient* fill and make this red and blue, or any alternatives that you prefer.

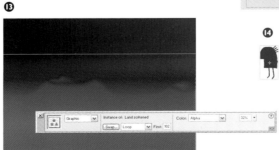

16

17

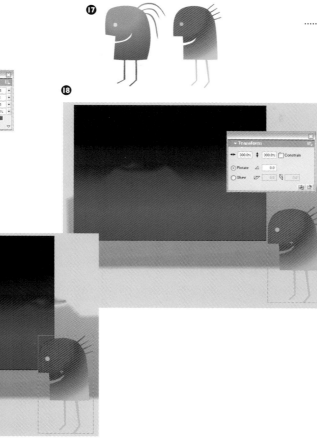

18

19

20

21

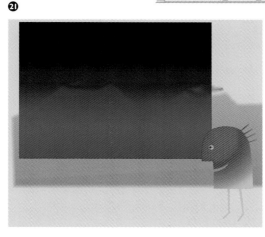

22

129

Ascent of Man

16 Repeat steps 14 and 15 for the Female, but choose a different colour radial gradient.

17 Draw circles for the eye 'whites' on both images. As the eyeballs will be animated, they should appear on their own separate layer.

18 Add a blank keyframe at frame 56 and drag an Instance of the Male symbol onstage, using the *Transform* panel to change the scaling to 300 per cent. Then drag the image offstage right.

19 Add a new keyframe at frame 64, and move the Male a little to the left so the eye is just visible.

20 Click in the area between keyframes 56 and 64 and add *Frame > Motion Tweening*, or *Tween > Motion* in Flash MX, with its default settings. Add two new keyframes at frames 89 and 97 and repeat the process in reverse, i.e. moving the image back to its original position offstage right, again adding motion tweening with default values.

21 Create a new layer above the others, calling it 'Eyes'. In a blank keyframe, use the Brush tool to draw a black eyeball. Go to *Insert > Convert to Symbol*, call it 'Eyeball', and set *Behavior* to *Graphic*.

22 Drag the keyframe to frame 61 and position the eyeball within the eye shape towards the left.

130

23 Add additional keyframes at frames 62, 63, 64 and 65 and move the eye shape to the left, corresponding to the Male layer beneath. This process is best seen using *Onion Skinning* in *Outline View*.

24 Add a keyframe at frame 72 and move the eyeball to the centre of the eye.

25 Add additional keyframes at frames 89, 90, 91 and 92, but move the eyeball around in an excited state (as the close-up details show). So far, then, the background images have been established; the male and female figures and the eyeballs have been created. The male image moves into frame and out again, with some manipulated eyeball movement.

26 Remember that at step 10 you dragged the enlarged Land Softened layer, so that most of the image appeared offstage right. Now you are going to pan this layer, moving it slowly across the screen towards the left while the excited male character is bouncing across the screen in the same direction. Return to the Land Softened layer and add a keyframe at frame 104 and another at frame 183. At 183, move the entire image offstage to the left. (Do this while in *Outline View* for clarity.)

27 Click in the area between keyframes 104 and 183 and add *Motion Tweening*, changing *Easing* to 40. This means that the tween will slow down towards the end.

28 At frame 144 the Land Softened layer has travelled to this position, which is about halfway across.

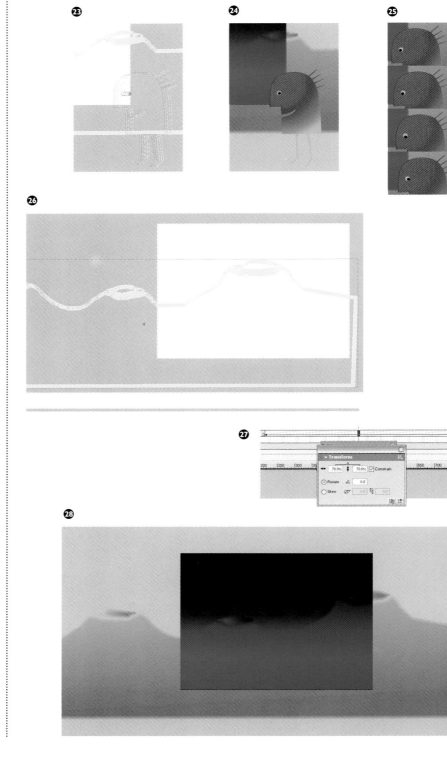

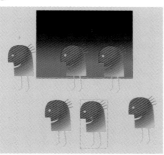

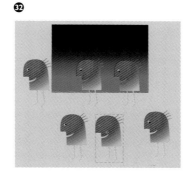

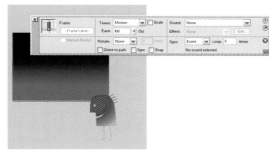

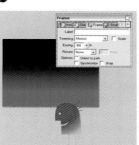

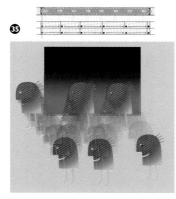

29 Return to the Male layer and add keyframes at frames 119, 126, 133, 141, 149 and 157. At frame 119 drag the image to a new offstage position. This will be the start point for his bounce.

30 Move to frame 126 and drag the image partially onstage.

31 Continue this process, moving the images up and down until frame 157 is reached. The six images should be in the positions shown here.

32 Return to the Eyes layer and add new keyframes in identical positions to those just added to the Male layer, i.e. at frames 119, 126, 133, 141, 149 and 157. Then reposition the eyeball as shown.

33 Now add *Motion Tweening* to both the Male and Eyes layers. As the character bounces up, his movement should decelerate towards the top of his bounce. Do this by setting *Easing* to 100.

34 As the character 'bounces down', his movement will decelerate towards the bottom of the bounce by setting *Easing* to –100.

35 The movement sequence and a detail of a section of the timeline looks like this when shown in *Onion Skin* mode.

132

❶ You should now repeat this sequence, but this time in the other direction. The character should travel faster now, so there are only five instead of seven frames between each step. The bounce is also more energetic and he almost reaches the top of the frame. In order to do all this, go to the Male layer and add a keyframe at frame 88. Use the *Transform* panel to change the *Skew* setting to 180, so he is facing stage right.

❷ Add keyframes at frames 194, 200, 206 and 212. Repeat the process on the Eyes layer, moving each eyeball to fit the eye. Add *Motion Tweening* between each with *Easing* values as described in steps 33 and 34. The movement sequence and a detail of the timeline just described looks like this when shown in *Onion Skin* mode.

❸ Now return to the Land Softened layer. Add a keyframe at frame 227. Remember that this image is still at 200 per cent scaling.

❹ Add a keyframe at frame 252, and use the *Transform* panel to change the scaling to 100 per cent and reposition the image. Use the *Effects* panel to alter the xA value to 143 using the slide. This has the effect of 'sharpening' the image by removing some of the softening that was applied at the beginning of the project.

❺ Add *Motion Tweening*, using its default values.

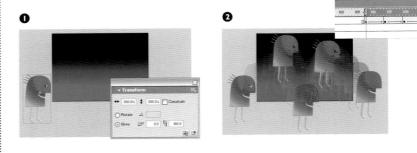

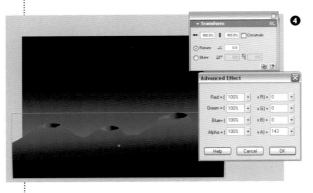

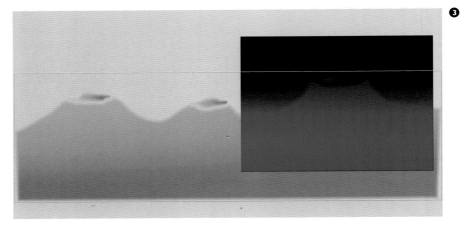

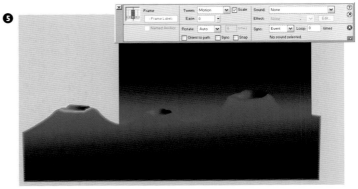

6 The Male, who will be joined onstage by the Female, will be bouncing out of craters. To enable this, an extra layer has to be created above (i.e. in front) of the characters. To do this, you should create the Land layer in front and add a blank keyframe at frame 275. Go to the *Library* panel to drag another Instance of the Land Softened symbol onstage. Use the *Subselect* tool to remove the craters. Add extra frames to this layer up to frame 462.

7 As the male character appears at two different sizes throughout the animation, it is best to place him on two layers. So add a new 'Male Small' layer below Land in front, and add a new keyframe at frame 275. From the *Library* panel drag another Instance of the Male symbol on stage and go to *Modify > **Transform*** to rescale the character to a convenient size. Position him just below the third crater. (This is best done in *Outline View* for clarity.)

8 Add a keyframe at frame 284 and move the character upwards.

9 Add a keyframe at frame 292 and move the character downwards again. Add three more keyframes at frames 300, 309 and 317 and repeat the process described in steps 7 and 8 (this page).

10 Add a keyframe at frame 326 and move the character to just below the middle crater. Add two more keyframes at frames 335 and 343 and repeat the process described in steps 7, 8 and 9 (this page).

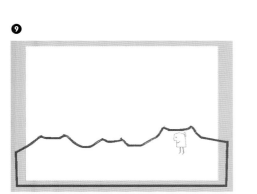

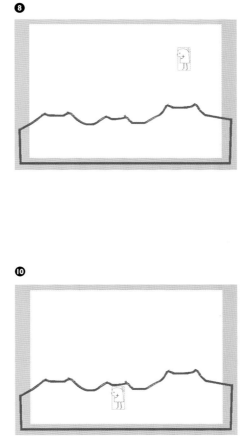

134

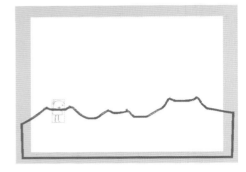

⓫ Add a keyframe at frame 353 and move the character to just below the left crater. Use the *Transform* panel to change the *Skew* setting to 180. He now faces stage right.

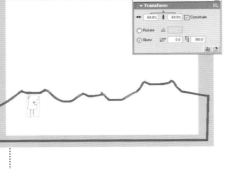

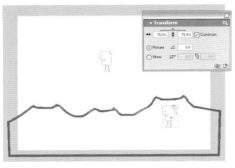

⓬ Finally add a keyframe at frame 357 and move the character so that he is just peeking out of the left crater. Click in the area between keyframes 353 and 357 and add *Motion Tweening*.

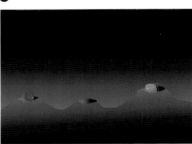

⓭ Now create a new layer named 'Female' below Male Small. Add a blank keyframe at frame 338 and drag an instance of the Female symbol onstage. Use the *Transform* panel to change the scaling to match the Male, at 70 per cent.

⓮ Add keyframes at frames 347, 355, 363, 371 and 379 and move the character up and down in the same way you did with the Male. However, at frame 379 you should position the Female so that she is just peeking out too. Add *Motion Tweening* with *Easing* as before. *Normal* view is now restored.

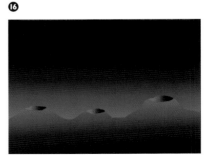

⓯ The next event in the sequence is the Female's head disappearing, which is closely followed by the Male's. They will both emerge again from the centre crater. So, return to the Female layer, add a keyframe at frame 395 and move her down out of sight.

⓰ Return to the Male Small layer, add a keyframe at frame 400 and move the character down out of sight.

⑰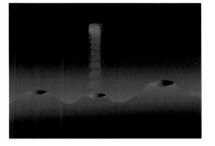

⑱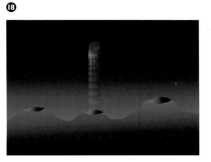

⑲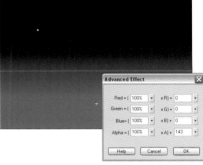

⑳

㉑

㉒

㉓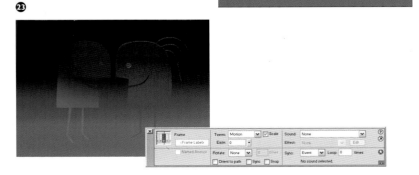

⑰ Return to the Female layer, add a keyframe at frame 409 and move the character to the centre crater and down out of sight. Add two more keyframes at frames 422 and 435 to move the character up and then down again. The *Onion Skin* view here shows part of the sequence.

⑱ Return to the Male Small layer, add keyframes at frames 435, 439 and 462 and repeat the same process just applied to the Female.

⑲ Return to the Land Softened layer, add keyframes at frames 473 and 488, and add *Motion Tweening*. At frame 488 use the *Effects* panel to reduce Alpha transparency and *xA* to 0 per cent.

⑳ Return to the Male Small layer, add a keyframe at frame 488 and use the *Transform* panel to change the scaling to 320 per cent. Position him just left of centre stage.

㉑ Return to the Female layer, add a keyframe at frame 488 and repeat the process just applied to the Male.

㉒ Add another keyframe at frame 491, then return to frame 488 and use the *Effects* panel to reduce Alpha transparency to 0 per cent. Add *Motion Tweening* and the image will rapidly appear.

㉓ Return to the Male Small layer, add a keyframe at frame 491 and repeat the process just applied to the Female. Then add a further four keyframes at frames 494, 498 and 502 – these are to correspond to the winking eye.

136

24 Return to the Eye layer and add the same four keyframes to this layer too. Position the eyeball within the eye shape, at frames 488 and 491, so both characters are looking at each other.

25 At frame 494 move the eyeballs to a central position, so they are now looking outwards.

26 At frame 498 replace the Male eyeball with a line drawn with the *Pen* tool. Frame 502 should remain the same as frame 494.

27 The only thing left to do is create the title. So add a new layer above all the others named 'Title'. Add a keyframe at frame 10 and use the *Text* tool to type the words 'Ascent of Man'. We used the Jokerman font selected from the Character panel. This used most of the default settings, except for text size (changed to 33 point) and the colour is now magenta R255/G0/B191. Use *Insert* > **Convert to Symbol** and name the new symbol 'Title'.

28 Add keyframes at frames 28, 43 and 56 and go to *Effects* > **Alpha Transparency**, or *Colour* > **Alpha** in Flash MX, and change this to 0 per cent on frames 10 and 56.

29 Between frames 10 and 28, and between 43 and 56, add *Motion Tweening* with default values. The title will then fade in, stay for 15 frames and then fade out.

That's it! 520 frames in eight layers. The steps opposite provide extra information.

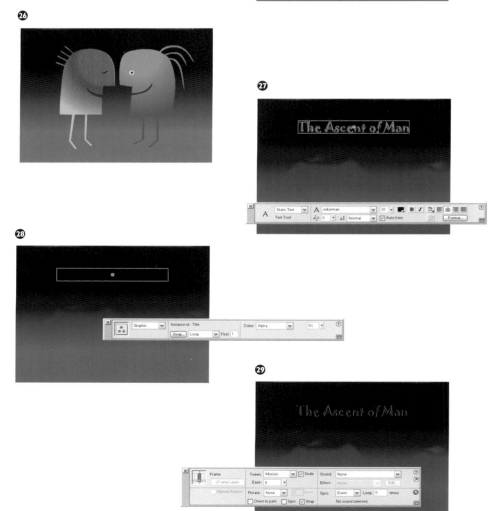

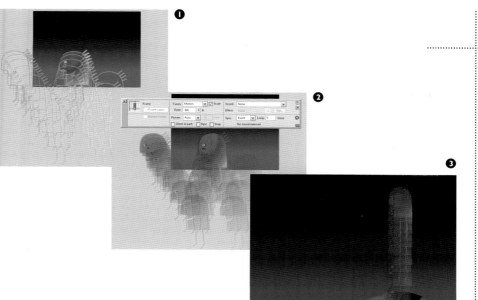

Checklist

❶ For the bouncing man, *Motion Tweening* takes care of the frames in between the keyframes.

❷ The eyeballs are also *Motion Tweened*, but you need to ensure that the *Easing* is set to the same value for both eyeballs (in the Male and Female characters) – otherwise the eyeballs will not synchronize with the eyes.

❸ To enable the characters to bounce up out of the craters, a copy of the Land Softened layer is made and named Land in Front. This is positioned above them. The craters on this layer are then deleted, to leave the Male and Female layers sandwiched between them.

❹ At frame 462 the Land in Front layer is no longer required, as the characters are no longer bouncing out of the craters.

❺ The conclusion of the animation is anticipated on frame 473 by the fading of the Land Softened layer to an Alpha transparency of 0 per cent.

❻ The two characters emerge from this using a very rapid three-frame tween: from 0 to 100 per cent in just three frames or 0.25 seconds.

❼ Finally, the wink is accomplished with a single line of the *Pencil* tool, which is set to the finest *Smooth* option.

138

THREE WAYS
TO LOSE WEIGHT

This project is completely made up of vector graphics and is only 43kb. It is split into four scenes, the introduction and the three 'ways'. Flash plays them in numerical order. Using multiple scenes like this enables you to treat each scene as a separate animation, which stops the timeline from getting too cluttered. In scene three, a sausage becomes a pig. This is done using *Shape Tweening*, but this can be used only to morph a single object into another single object. For all the other sequences, you must therefore use frame-by-frame animation.

All objects are drawn directly in Flash. The face, the two sausages and the steam are all converted into symbols because *Motion Tweening* will be applied to them. A new keyframe is inserted each time an object is repeated. The features of the face are distorted for each frame. Although it is time-consuming, frame-by-frame animation gives you total control over the frame content. In a complex animation, *Onion Skinning* may help you to see the frame progression, or you can move back and forth to check that the sequence is working by using the controller or the keyboard arrow keys. Try simulating the facial expressions using a mirror before drawing them. See if you can add extra ideas to this project too – five or even 10 ways to lose weight will make a satisfying, yet still short, cartoon.

Plan out all the scenes before you start so that the head position can remain constant for each. To do this, try out different head drawings until you find one that you are happy with. The frame rate should be lowered to seven from the default of 12 so the animation is slowed down a little. A higher frame rate would require more frames to be drawn for each sequence, but would result in a smoother animation. The hair remains unchanged while all other features vary from frame to frame. Even though the drawing style is very basic, try to express emotions in the face. For example, the features should move upwards as the rubber approaches, the mouthless face should wriggle as if to say, 'Where is my mouth?', and the lips pucker as she is about to suck the straw. Use *Modify > Optimize* to reduce the number of anchor points in all the shapes to simplify the animation and reduce the file size. Doing this will also make editing the shapes a lot easier.

❶

❷

T I P

Objects of desire

To ensure that you create a single object for *Shape Tweening*, start with an ellipse and use the *Shape* tool to distort it into roughly the shape you require. You can use the *Arrow* tool initially, then add anchor points using the *Pen* tool and finally drag those anchor points into the desired position using the *Subselect* tool.

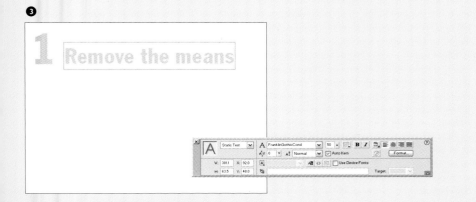

❸

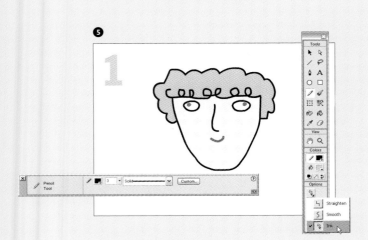

Scenes 1 and 2

❶ Using the default movie size of 550 x 400 pixels, create a layer named 'Ways…' Use the *Text* tool to type the title. The example uses the font Franklin Gothic Condensed, selected from the *Character* panel. This uses the default setting, but the text size was changed to 50 point and the colour is now maroon R153/G0/B151. Use the same settings for the number '3', but increase its size to 100 point. Position both layers stage left.

❷ Go to *Windows > Panels > Scene* (*Windows > Scene* in Flash MX), click '+', and scene two will be added, along with a fresh stage with an empty timeline.

❸ Create a new layer named 'Title'. At keyframe 1 add the text using the same character settings that you used for scene one, but change the colour to beige R230/G213/B155.

❹ Add a keyframe at frame 16 and delete the title to leave just the number 1, which will persist throughout the scene.

❺ Create a new layer named 'Face', below the Title layer. Create a blank keyframe at frame 16. Using the *Pencil* tool set to *Ink*, which allows a more flexible drawing style, draw the face using a constant three-pixel black stroke (outline). Fill this with colours of your choice. Next, go to *Insert > Convert to Symbol*, call it 'Face', and set *Behavior* to *Graphic*. This image will be used for frame-by-frame animation, and so will not be tweened, so it is not strictly necessary to convert it to a symbol, but it is usually convenient to store any often-used item in the *Library*.

140

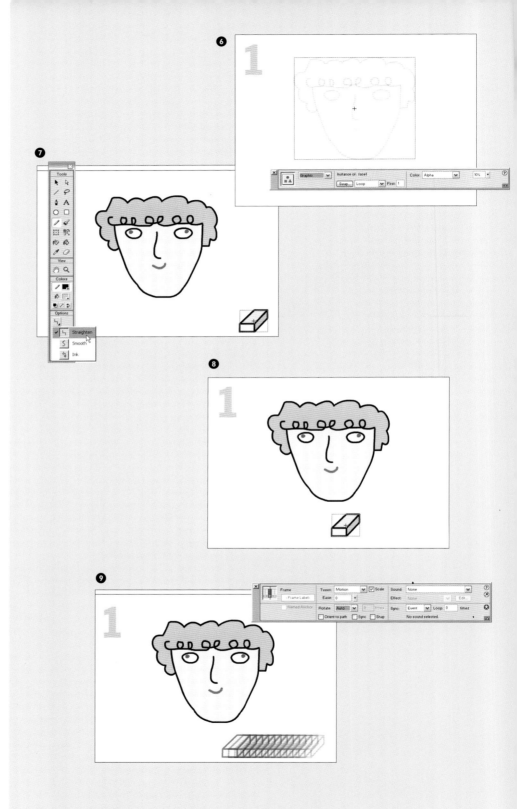

6 At frame 21 add another keyframe and then return to frame 16 to reduce Alpha transparency to 10 per cent. This establishes the ghosted image for five frames before switching to the full-strength image at frame 21.

7 Create a new layer named 'Rubber' above the Face layer. Add another keyframe at frame 27. Using the *Pencil* tool set to *Straighten*, which constrains the drawing style to straight lines, draw the rubber using a constant three-pixel black stroke (outline). Fill this with the colours of your choice. Move the image to the bottom right of the stage. Convert this into a graphic.

8 For the next sequence of frames, the Rubber will move over the Face and rub out the mouth. To simplify these instructions, you should establish all the Rubber positions first and then move onto the Face layer so the facial expressions react to the Rubber. Therefore, start by adding another keyframe at frame 40 and move the Rubber to the left.

9 Go to *Frame > Motion Tweening*, or *Tween > Motion* in Flash MX, and select its default settings. An *Onion Skinning* view will show you that the intermediate frames have been automatically created.

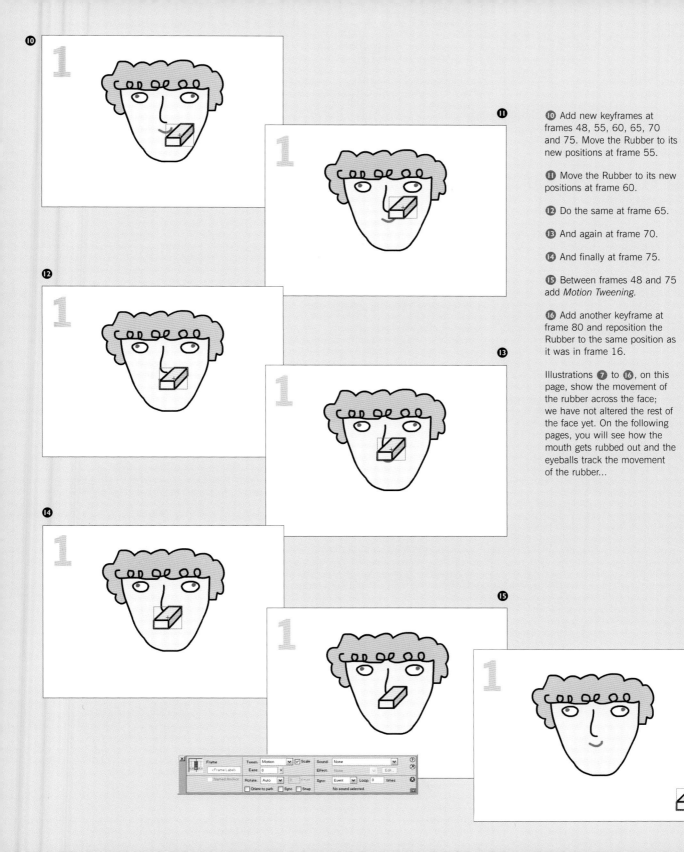

10 Add new keyframes at frames 48, 55, 60, 65, 70 and 75. Move the Rubber to its new positions at frame 55.

11 Move the Rubber to its new positions at frame 60.

12 Do the same at frame 65.

13 And again at frame 70.

14 And finally at frame 75.

15 Between frames 48 and 75 add *Motion Tweening*.

16 Add another keyframe at frame 80 and reposition the Rubber to the same position as it was in frame 16.

Illustrations **7** to **16**, on this page, show the movement of the rubber across the face; we have not altered the rest of the face yet. On the following pages, you will see how the mouth gets rubbed out and the eyeballs track the movement of the rubber...

142

⑰ Now return to the Face and edit the eyes, nose, mouth and facial outline. The hair remains constant throughout, so add keyframes at frames 27, 34, 40, 55, 60, 65, 70, 75, 83, 85, 87, 89, 91 and 93. At frame 27 the eyeballs move to bottom right, as they have noticed the Rubber, and at the same time lips flatten and move up slightly while the nose puckers.

⑱ Continue making the facial alterations at frame 34.

⑲ Continue making the facial alterations at frame 40.

⑳ And again at 55.

㉑ And at 60.

㉒ At 65.

㉓ At 70.

㉔ At 75.

㉕ At frame 83 the mouth is fully erased, so ensure there is some facial wriggling.

㉖ Continue making the facial alterations at 85.

㉗ Continue making the facial alterations at 87.

㉘ And again at 89.

㉙ At 91.

㉚ And finally at frame 93.

Now add extra frames on all the layers up to frame 105.

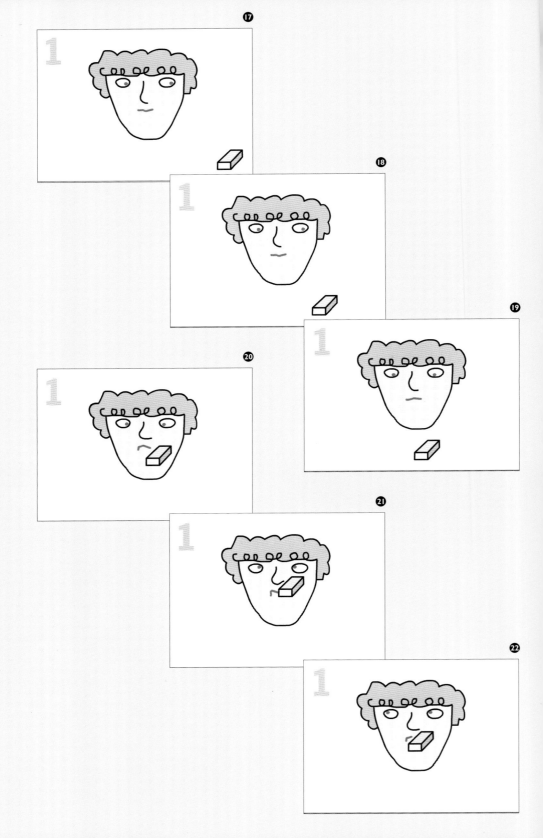

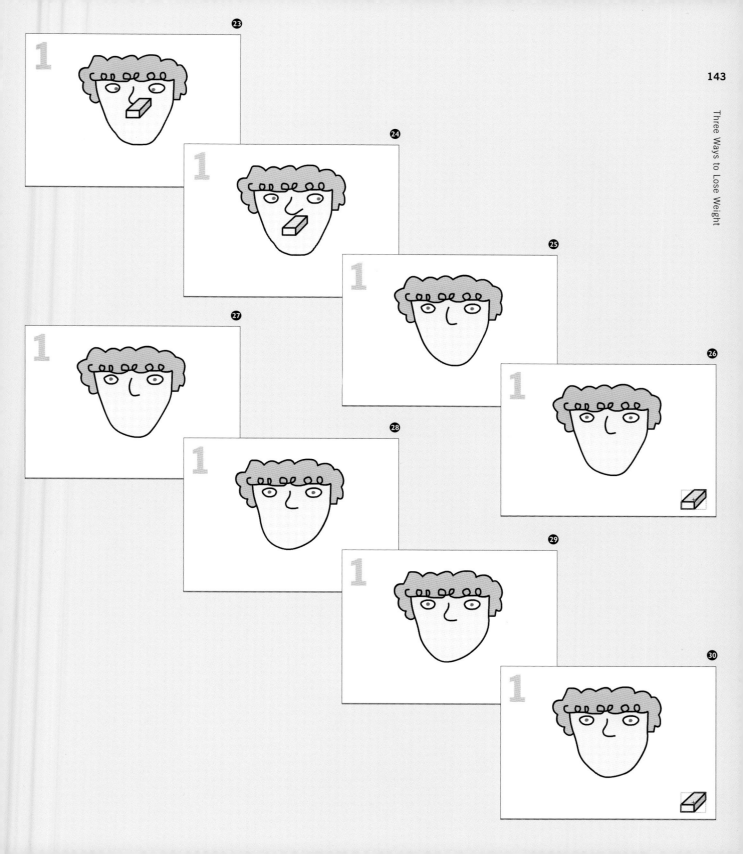

144   ## Scene 3

❶ Click on *Windows > Select Panels > Scene > '+'* and Scene 3 will be added along with a fresh stage and an empty timeline. Add a layer named 'Title' plus keyframes at frames 1 and 16 and repeat the process of adding the title as you did previously.

❷ Create a new layer named 'Face' below the Title layer. From the *Library* panel drag another Instance of the Face symbol onstage and drag the resulting keyframe to frame 16.

❸ At frame 21 add another keyframe and then return to frame 16. Go to *Effects > **Alpha Transparency**, or Colour > **Alpha*** in Flash MX, and reduce it to 10 per cent. This establishes the ghosted image for five frames, before switching to the full-strength image at frame 21.

❹ Create a new layer named 'Glass and Fruit' above the Face layer and add a keyframe at frame 21. Use the *Pencil* tool set to a *Stroke* weight of three pixels and draw the glass. Then switch to the *Brush* tool and add some coloured blobs (fruit).

❺ Create a new layer named 'Ice Cream' above the Face layer, but beneath the Glass and Fruit layer and add a keyframe at frame 21. Use the *Brush* tool to add some ice cream in pastel colours. The idea here is for the ice cream to drain away out of the glass and for the face to react to this situation.

⑥

⑦

⑧

⑨

⑩

⑪

⑥ To create this, start with the glass. Add keyframes at frames 34, 40 and 45 to both the Glass and Fruit and Ice Cream layers. At frame 34 edit the shapes and remove the elements altogether so that they appear lower down the glass.

⑦ At frame 40 edit the shapes again.

⑧ At frame 45 edit the shapes again until there is a small amount of ice cream. For the purposes of the example shown here, we used just four keyframes to complete this process. If you add additional keyframes to provide intermediate steps, you will get a smoother animation.

⑨ Next create a new layer named 'Straw' above the Face and Ice Cream layers, but below the Glass and Fruit layer. Add a keyframe at frame 21, then use the *Pencil* tool to add two blue lines, making the one on the right slightly darker.

⑩ Add keyframes to the Straw layer at frames 28 and 34 and to the Face layer at frames 28, 34, 40 and 45. At frame 28 purse the lips, pucker the nose, move the eyeballs down to look at the ice cream, and move the straw to the lips.

⑪ At frame 34 'flare' the nose, open the mouth and the eyes in astonishment, and allow the straw to fall away.

146

12 At frame 40 the mouth should be downturned, the nose sharpened and the eyes heavy. The straw remains static.

13 At frame 45 the mouth is downturned and thin, the nose drooping and the eyes drooping as well, but still the straw remains static.

14 The action now moves down to the area beneath the glass so that the viewer can see where the ice cream has gone. To create this, the elements on stage must be moved upwards. At frame 50 add keyframes to all layers (except the Title layer). Move the face, the glass and the straw upwards so that just the chin is visible onstage. On the Glass and Fruit layer, change the colour of the glass to grey and add two bands of colour to indicate a tabletop and a floor. On the Ice Cream layer, use the same colours to create a pyramid of ice cream on the floor. On the Straw layer, extend the bottom of the straw to the top of the ice cream 'pyramid'.

15 The remaining action takes place on the Ice Cream layer, so add keyframes at frames 52, 54, 56 and 58; at frame 52 extend the ice cream pyramid.

16 At frame 54 extend the ice cream pyramid.

17 At frame 56 extend the ice cream pyramid.

18 At frame 58 extend the ice cream pyramid.

Now add extra frames on all layers up to frame 75.

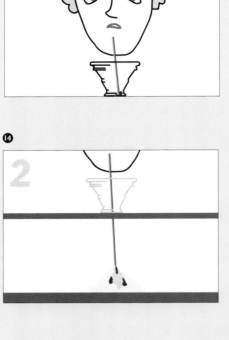

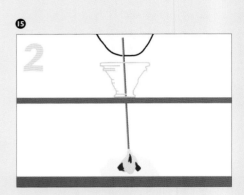

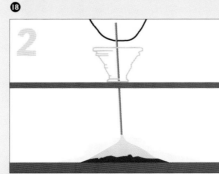

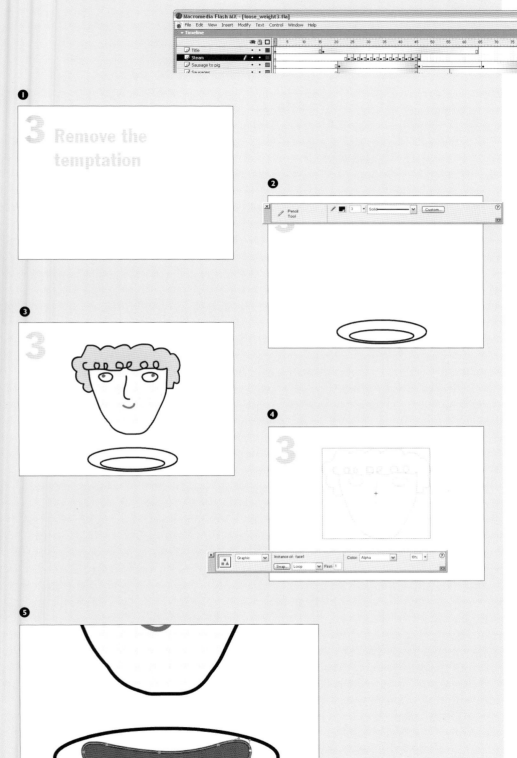

Scene 4

❶ Click on *Windows* > *Panels* > *Scene* (*Windows* > **Scene** in Flash MX) and scene 4 will be added along with a fresh stage with an empty timeline. Add a layer called 'Title', make keyframes at frames 1 and 16, and repeat the process of adding the Title as you did in the previous scenes.

❷ Add a new layer named 'Plate' and put a keyframe in at frame 21. Use the *Stroke* panel to set the line weight to three pixels. Then use the *Oval* tool to draw two ellipses to form the plate.

❸ Create a new layer named 'Face' below the Title layer. Drag another Instance of the Face symbol onstage and drag the resulting keyframe to frame 16.

❹ At frame 21 add another keyframe and then return to frame 16. Go to *Effects* > **Alpha Transparency**, or *Colour* > **Alpha** in Flash MX, and reduce it to 10 per cent. This establishes the ghosted image for five frames before switching to the full-strength image at frame 21 as before.

❺ Next you need to create a sausage. Add a new layer named 'Sausage to Pig' and add a keyframe at frame 21. Use the *Pencil* tool with the *Stroke* set to three pixels to draw the sausage outline. Refine the shape using the *Subselect* tool, and when you are satisfied fill it with brown – try R190/G85/B61. At a later keyframe this sausage will morph into a pig, using *Shape Tweening*. Unlike in *Motion Tweening*, symbols cannot be used for *Shape Tweening*.

148

⑥ Only one sausage can morph into the pig, but this animation requires two more. So add a new layer named 'Two Sausages' below the Sausage to Pig layer, and add a keyframe at frame 21. Paste two copies of the sausage and adjust the positions. These two will appear behind the other one, since they are on a layer beneath it. These two sausages will appear later as a *Motion Tween*, so use *Insert* > **Convert to Symbol**, call it 'Two Sausages', and set *Behavior* to *Graphic*.

⑦ Add a new layer called 'Steam' and add a keyframe at frame 28. From the *Tools* panel use the *Brush* at its largest size with an oblique shape, and set the colour to beige R230/G213/B155. Draw a steam shape.

⑧ Select *Modify* > **Optimize** to reduce the number of anchor points that make up the shape. Always check the complexity of shapes created in Flash because they increase file size and playback performance.

⑨ Now select *Modify* > *Shape* > **Soften Fill Edges** and change the settings to *Distance* 8 pixels, *Steps* 4 and *Direction,* to *Expand*.

⑩ Copy the image and paste it three times, positioning the images as shown here. The softened shape will look like this. Create a new graphic symbol called 'Steam'.

⑪ Add additional keyframes at two-frame intervals starting at frame 32 and finishing at frame 56. On every other keyframe, drag another Instance of Steam onstage. Return to frame 32 and reduce Alpha transparency to 11 per cent.

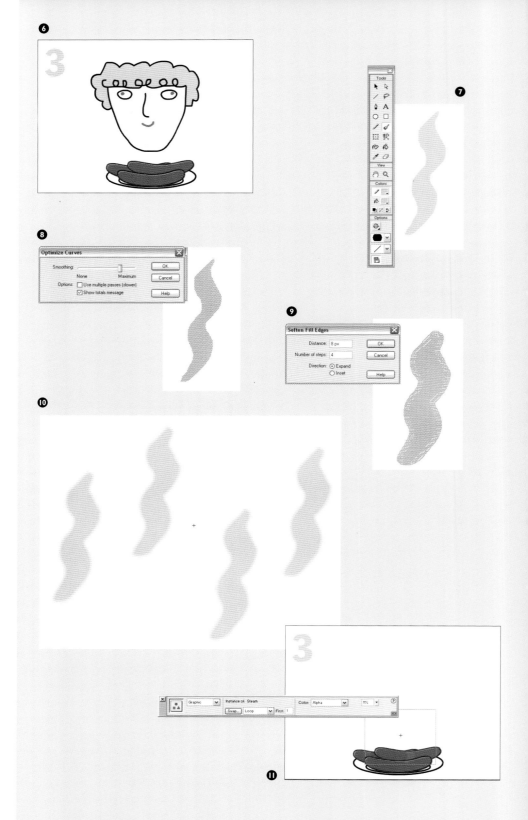

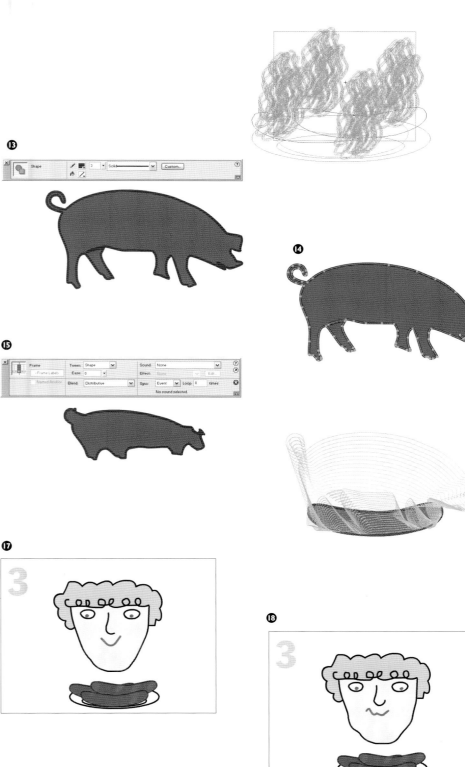

12 On all subsequent keyframes of Steam, vary the Alpha transparency to between 7 and 20 per cent and shift the Steam object a little so that it is not identical frame-to-frame. The effect is best shown in *Onion Skin* mode viewed as *Outlines*.

13 Now return to the Sausage to Pig layer and add a keyframe at frame 60. Add another keyframe at frame 80, but make it a blank keyframe. Using the *Pencil* tool, set to a *Stroke* of three pixels, draw the pig shape. It must be a single continuous outline shape with no breaks, and avoid the lines crossing each other. It is possible to paste a copy of the sausage and drag it by its anchor points into the shape of a pig; this way you can ensure that the shape is continuous.

14 Use the *Subselect* tool to refine the shape using the anchor points.

15 Add *Shape Tweening*, keeping its default values.

16 The entire tween is shown using *Onion Skin* view and *Outline* mode.

17 Now return to the Face layer. Add keyframes at the following frames: 28, 31, 34, 37, 40, 43, 46, 49, 62, 65, 68, 71, 74, 77, 80 and 83. Frames 28 to 49 show the face anticipating food. Starting at frame 28, move the eyeballs down to look at the sausages, pucker the nose and curve the mouth upwards.

18 On frame 31 continue to adjust the features with the additional puckering of the face outline.

150

19 On frame 34 continue as you did in the previous step.

20 On frame 37 continue to adjust the features.

21 On frame 40 continue to adjust the features.

22 On frame 43 continue to adjust the features.

23 On frame 46 continue to adjust the features.

24 On frame 49 continue to adjust the features.

25 Frames 62 to 83 show the face become startled and then disappointed as the sausage becomes a pig. Starting at frame 62, continue to adjust the features – the most important thing is to start opening the mouth.

26 On frame 65 continue to adjust the features.

27 On frame 68 continue to adjust the features.

28 On frame 71 continue to adjust the features.

29 On frame 74 continue to adjust the features.

30 On frame 77 continue to adjust the features.

31 On frame 80 continue to adjust the features.

32 On frame 83 continue to adjust the features.

Now add extra frames on all the layers up to frame 102 to complete the animation.

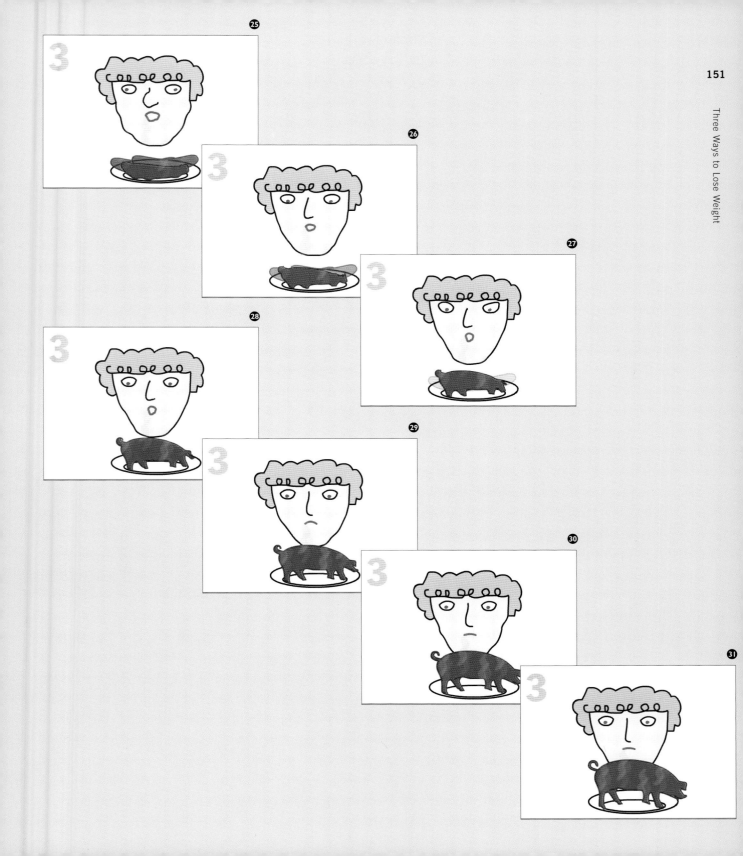

152 WORDS

'Words' is a 750-frame project, which is over a
minute of animation but is still only 43kb. Like
'Three Ways to Lose Weight', this is divided into
four scenes, the introduction, and three mini-
animations based on the words Death, Time and
Birth. You may, of course, prefer to use alternative
words or add in some extras, but the key feature
here is the transition between the scenes. The
background colour at the end of each scene is
designed to blend with the beginning of the next,
and the third scene loops back to the introduction.

Most of these colour changes are created using
*Effects > **Advanced***. This is the most useful tool for
manipulating colour in Flash. In fact, you could
create just black objects initially and then apply
colour to each Instance. Tweening is used here too.
The Intro features letters falling onto a fine white
line, each in a slightly different way. You should
always start from where you want to end up, to
space out the letters on the line correctly. Each will
need to be converted to a symbol before you add
any keyframes and tweening.

A large number of graphic symbols are created,
so it is convenient to store them in separate folders
in the *Library*. Don't worry if you move a symbol
from one folder to another because Flash will
automatically link it to the existing instances.
The scenes used for the three words should be
created sequentially in order to control the colour
transitions between them. The exception is scene
one, the introduction.

TIP

Colour sampling faults in Flash

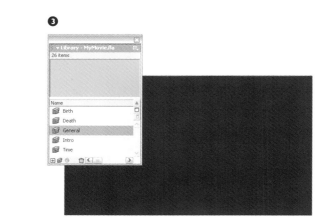

Flash does have some infuriating idiosyncrasies;
one is the use of the *Dropper* tool to sample a
colour. If the colour of an object has been
changed using the *Advanced Effects* panel, the
dropper will not be able to sample the resulting
colour. If you want to apply the colour to a new
object, you will have to use a screen grab utility
to capture that portion of the screen, paste it
into a new Flash document (which is discarded
later), and sample the colour here.

❶

❷

❸

④

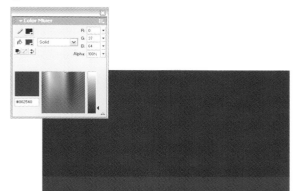

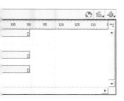

⑤

⑥

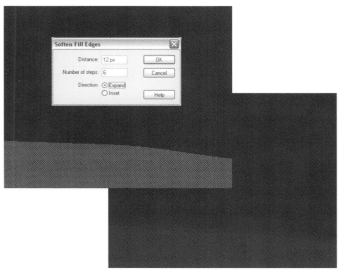

Scene 2: Death

① Use *Movie Properties* to establish a movie size of 550 x 320 pixels.

② The *Layers* panel detail here shows the six layers and the completed timeline used in the scene.

③ The first task is to create the background and foreground. On a layer named 'Background' draw a rectangle to cover the entire stage area. Set *Stroke* to *Nil* and fill it with dark blue R0/G5/B51. Convert this into a symbol, naming it 'Variable Ground'. Store this in a new folder named 'General'. This folder will be used for all the symbols that are used in multiple scenes.

④ Create a new layer named 'Foreground', draw a rectangle 550 x 70 pixels with nil *Stroke*, and fill this with grey blue R0/G41/B72. Position it at the bottom of the stage.

⑤ Drawing on top of this image, create a shape that is wavy at the top using the *Arrow* and/or *Subselect* tool to adjust the shape, adding anchor points with the *Pen* tool.

⑥ Use *Modify > Shape > Soften Fill Edges*, with the settings: *Distance* 12, *Steps* 6 and *Direction* Expand to create a vignette border to the rectangle.

154

7 With *Fill* set to RGB 0/37/64 (Web colour 002540), use the *Brush* tool with an oblique shape and draw a shape with a jagged top edge that covers most of the rectangle. Use the *Arrow* or *Subselect* tool to adjust the shape, adding anchor points with the *Pen* tool.

8 Use the *Arrow* tool to trim off from the sides and bottom any unwanted soft edge or excess from the jagged shape.

9 Create a new folder in the *Library* called 'Death' and convert this image to a symbol saved in this new folder.

10 At this stage, the image should look something like this.

11 Go to the *Library* window and click '+' to add a new symbol, and call it 'DEATH'. Set the word DEATH in a sans serif font such as Futura Condensed, in the midblue RGB 0/105/140 (Web colour 00698C), size 50 point. Use *Modify > **Break Apart*** to change the text from a font to a graphic.

12 As the 'T' morphs into a cross, two images are required – one, 'DEA H', and the other, 'T'. So copy the word 'DEATH' and *Edit > **Paste in Place*** a new symbol named 'T'. Remove the unwanted letters from each symbol.

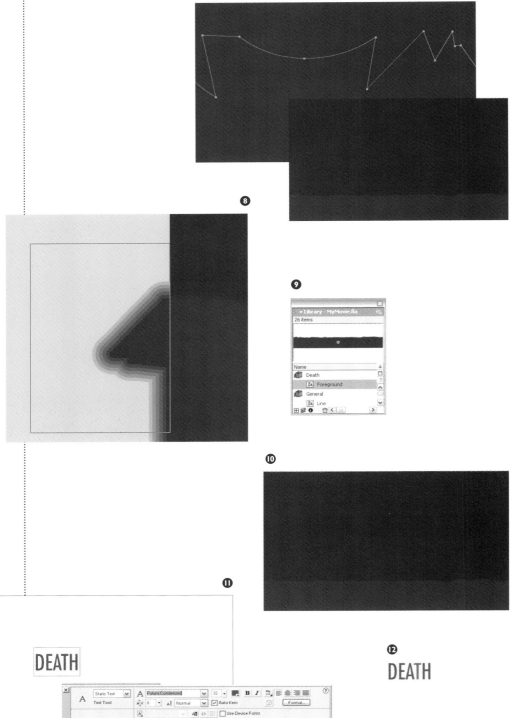

13 Create a new layer 'DEA H' and drag the symbol onstage to the desired position and move the keyframe to frame 11. Repeat the process with 'T' on another new layer.

14 On both these layers add a new keyframe at frame 34. Then return to the keyframes at frame 11 and make them transparent by setting *Frame > Effects > Alpha Transparency*, or *Colour > Alpha* in Flash MX's *Properties* window, to 0 per cent.

15 On both these layers click in the area between the keyframes and add *Frame > Effects > Motion Tween*, or *Tween > Motion* in Flash MX, using the default settings. The word DEATH, although distributed on two layers, now gradually emerges out of the blue background.

16 The next task is to turn the T into a cross, so add two keyframes on the T layer at frames 49 and 70.

17 At the keyframe for frame 70, use *View > Zoom In*, which will enable you to add four anchor points to the T. Then drag the outline so that it becomes a cross shape.

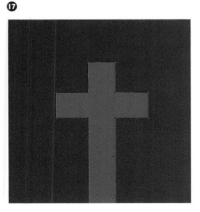

18 Now click in the area between keyframes 49 and 70 and use *Frame > Shape Tweening > Angular*, or *Tween > Shape*, and *Blend > Angular* from the *Properties* window in Flash MX, to add the *Shape Tween*.

19

19 At frame 49 go to *Modify > Transform > **Add Shape Hint** (Modify > Shape > **Shape Hint** in Flash MX), and a small red letter 'a' will appear. Drag this to the desired position (maximum zoom will help do this accurately). Then go to frame 70 and position the 'a' on this keyframe to the equivalent position on the altered letter. When the *Shape Hints* are correctly positioned, they will change to yellow on the keyframe at the start of the tween, and green on the second keyframe. Good *Shape Tweening* can be difficult to accomplish in Flash – trial and error and a good deal of patience will be necessary.

20 At frames 89, 91 and 94 add keyframes to layer T. Use *Modify > Transform > **Rotate** progressively to make the 'cross' lean to the right. In Flash MX, just pick the *Free Transform* tool or use the *Transform* window. Use the *Arrow* tool to adjust the position.

21 The final component of this scene is the comet. Add a new symbol and call it comet.

22 To create the white glow, first set the *Fill* to a *Radial Blend* of white to the dark blue R0/G5/B51 so that the outer part blends into the background. Ensure *Stroke* is set to *Nil*.

23 Use the *Oval* tool to draw a shallow ellipse.

24 Employ the *Transform Fill Button* to squash the blend into a similar shape to the oval.

20

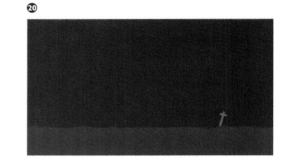

21

22

23

24

25 Adjust the size and drag the white epicentre right towards the head of the comet.

26 Use the *Subselect* tool to sharpen the tail of the comet.

27 Create a new layer named 'Comet' and drag the Comet symbol to position it just offstage in the top left. Move the resulting keyframe to frame 73.

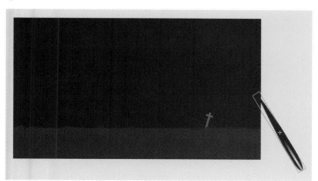

28 Create a keyframe at frame 94 and drag this Instance of Comet to the bottom right, just offstage. Use the *Transform* panel to change the scaling to 200 per cent.

29 The comet should travel on a path between these two keyframes so click in the space between them and add *Motion Tweening*. Ensure that the three path-related options are selected but that *Easing* and *Rotate* are set to *None*.

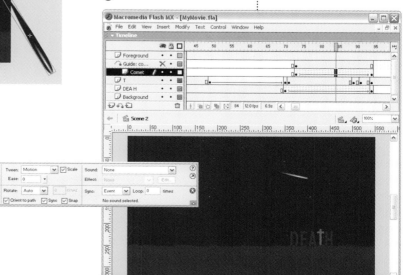

158

30 Now use *Insert > Motion Guide* so that a new guide layer will appear above the Comet layer.

31 On this new guide layer use the *Pencil* tool to draw the path of the comet, starting at the registration point of the Comet symbol at frame 73. The registration point is the little symbol at the centre – shown here in *Outline View*.

32 Draw the path towards its destination, which is the registration point of the Comet Instance at frame 94. You will not be able to see the Comet Instance at frame 94, so a rough position will do for now.

33 Return to the Comet layer at frame 94 and drag the Comet instance by its registration point to the end of the *Motion Guide* – you will see that it snaps to the end of the guide.

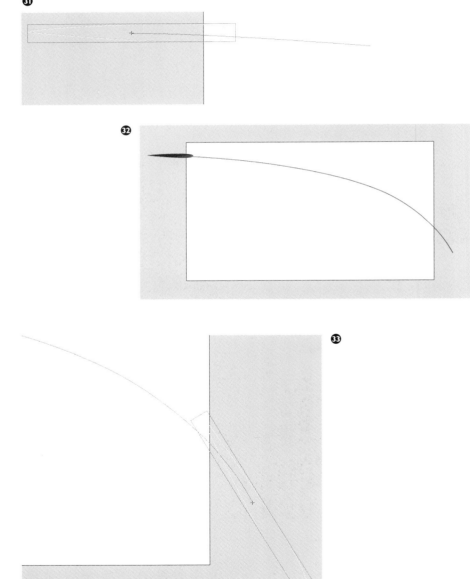

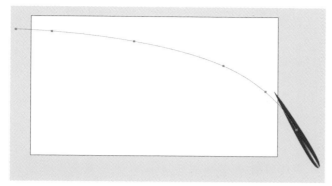

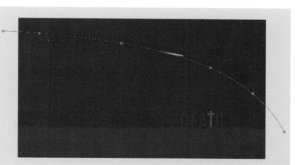

34 Use *Modify > Transform > **Rotate*** or pick the *Free Transform* tool to align the comets to their path. You can refine the shape of the *Motion Guide* using the *Subselect* tool and improve the positions of the comets until they are all satisfactory.

35 Add 15 blank frames to the end of the Foreground and Background layers to add a pause before the start of the next scene.

36 Use *Show/Hide Layers* to make the comet guide visible – it will not appear when you export the final animation.

37 This is the first scene that you are creating for this animation, but once the introduction is added later it will become Scene 2. Flash plays scenes in numerical order unless they are controlled by an Action. So use *Windows > Panels > **Scenes*** (*Windows > **Scenes*** in Flash MX) to rename this as 'Scene 2'.

38 Before you start the next scene, go to the last frame, 110, and select three objects: Foreground, Background and T. Copy them; they will be used at the start of the next scene.

160 Scene 3: Time

❶ Open the Scene window and click '+' to add a new scene, naming it 'Scene 3'.

❷ On layer 1 use *Edit* > *Paste in Place* to add the images from the final scene. Rename this layer 'Last Frame of Death'.

❸ Create a new folder in the *Library* for this scene, calling it 'Time'. Convert the images that you have just pasted into one symbol, giving it the same name as the layer. A symbol can contain multiple images, but they have to remain grouped if they are to be used again as an Instance.

❹ At frame 33 add a new keyframe. Enlarge this Instance to 250 per cent using the *Transform* panel. Ensure that *Constrain* is selected and then reposition the image. To see the stage area behind this image, go to *View* and select *Outlines* and *Work Area*.

❺ Go to *Effects* > *Advanced*, or *Colour* > *Advanced* from the Properties window in Flash MX, to change the colour to orange. Insert frames up to frame 72.

❻ Create a new layer above called 'Orange Ground' and drag an Instance of the Variable Ground symbol onstage. Position this using the *Info* panel, setting the x and y positions to 0 so that it covers the entire stage.

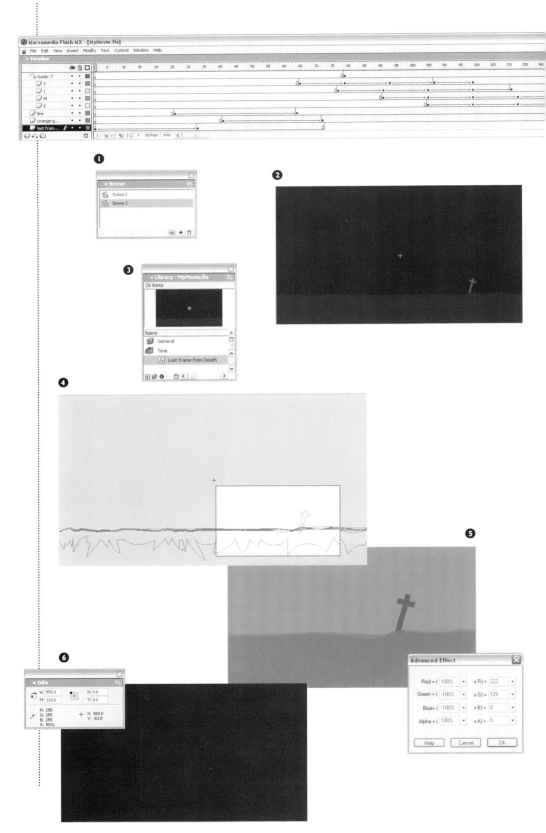

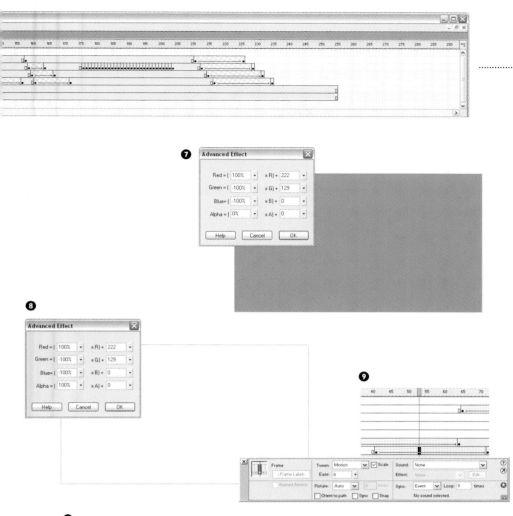

7 Drag the keyframe that has just been automatically created to frame 41. Use *Effects* > **Advanced**, or *Colours* > **Advanced** in MX, to change the Instance colour to orange.

8 Now create a new keyframe at frame 72, return to frame 41, and use *Effects* > *Advanced*, or *Colours* > **Advanced** in MX to change the Alpha transparency setting to 0 per cent. The existing settings in this panel are the ones that changed the original dark blue symbol to orange.

9 Click in the area between the two keyframes and select *Frames* > *Effects* > **Motion Tween**, or *Tween* > **Motion** in Flash MX, using the default settings.

10 Create a new layer above for the white line, calling it 'Line'. Use the *Pencil* tool on its *Hairline* setting to draw the line. Make it slightly wider than the stage, 556 pixels – this will make it easier to move it around. Convert this to a symbol and store it in the *General* folder because it will be reused in other scenes. A white graphic will, of course, not be visible on the white *Library* background, so to see it you need to change to *Outline View*. Position 'Line' vertically so that the base of the cross in the Last Frame of Death layer sits on it. A new symbol can either be created in the *Library* environment and then dragged onstage, or created onstage and then converted to a symbol – the choice is yours.

162

⓫ Drag the keyframe to frame 26 and then add another keyframe at frame 64. Return to frame 26 and move the Line Instance to the left until it is offstage. Select *View > **Outlines*** to see the stage area.

⓬ Click in the area between the two keyframes and add *Motion Tweening*, changing its *Easing* setting to 100 so that the movement begins fast and finishes more slowly. To summarize what you have done in this scene: the dark blue image with the cross appears, gradually gets bigger and changes to orange. At the same time, an orange panel appears that gradually obliterates this image, while above all this a white line moves onstage from the left. The next task is to introduce the four letters of the word 'TIME' in a staggered sequence. This is to allow each character to fly off to a new location while rotating and reducing in size. Each letter will follow the same motion guide that you will create later.

⓭ Start by creating the four letters in the *Library*. Click the '+' sign and use the *Text* tool to type the letter T. Try using the font Times New Roman selected from the *Character* panel, changing the text size to 120 pixels, and coloured black.

⓮ Continue creating the other three symbols for 'I', 'M', and 'E' in the same way.

⓯ Create a new layer above the existing ones, and call it 'T'. Drag the T symbol onstage and then move the keyframe that has been automatically created to frame 41 and align it with the cross so that it is sitting on the white line. Now move this keyframe to frame 79 – the cross is no longer visible.

⓫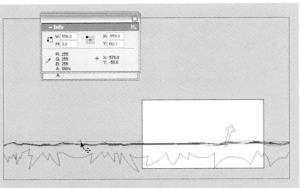

⓬

⓭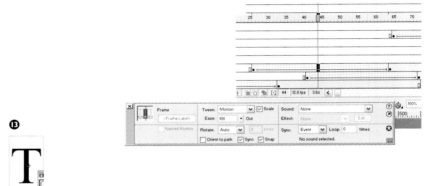

⓮

⓯

⑯

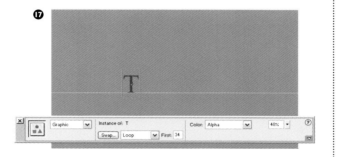

⑰

⑱

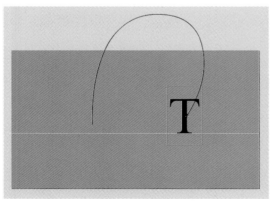

⑯ Add a keyframe at frame 107. Use the *Transform* panel to rescale the image down to 50 per cent.

⑰ Reduce the Alpha transparency to 40 per cent and move the T to the left, but make sure that it still sits on the line.

⑱ Use *Insert > **Motion Guide*** and a new guide layer will appear on top.

⑲ On this new layer use the *Pencil* tool to draw a semi-circular path leaning slightly to the right, and starting at the registration point of the T symbol at frame 79. Stop this roughly where you want the letter to end up.

⑳ Return to frame 107 and adjust the end of the motion guide so that it snaps to the registration point of the letter. When a guide layer is created, Flash adds frames up to the position of the first keyframe of the layer beneath. You can extend these frames to any number so that the path remains visible; it won't affect the actual path at all.

⑲

⑳

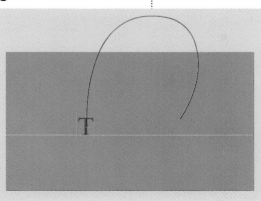

164

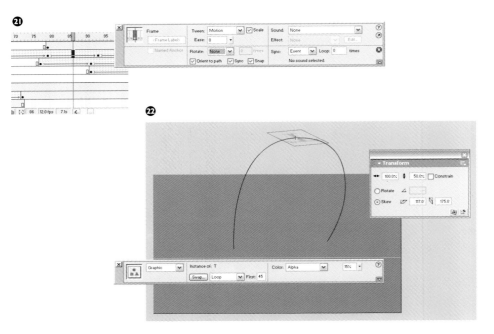

21 Now click in the area between frames 79 and 107 and add *Motion Tweening*, ensuring that the *Options* and *Scale* boxes are selected.

22 Add a new keyframe in the middle of the tween at frame 93. Use the *Transform* panel to skew and flatten this image to 50 per cent. Also reduce Alpha transparency to 15 per cent.

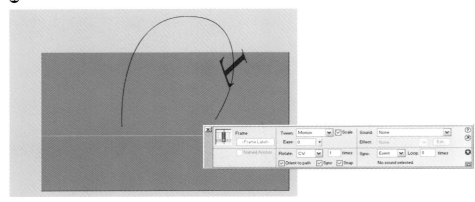

23 Now click in the area of the tween between frames 79 and 93. Add *Frame > Rotate > CW 1 Time*. In Flash MX this is done in the *Properties* window.

24 Now click in the area of the tween between frames 93 and 107 and add *Rotate > CCW 1 Time*.

25 The letter T now animates along a roughly semicircular path from right to left. It rotates clockwise until about halfway offstage, is distorted and continues to rotate, this time anti-clockwise, while all the time reducing in size and opacity. Although part of the animation is offstage, this *Onion Skin* image shows that the effect will be seen in the tween as it reappears. The T now has to fade in and out before it animates.

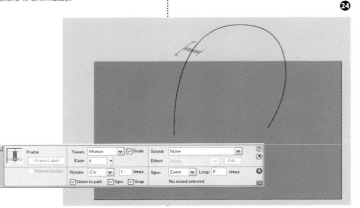

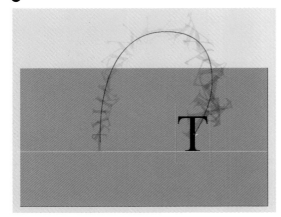

26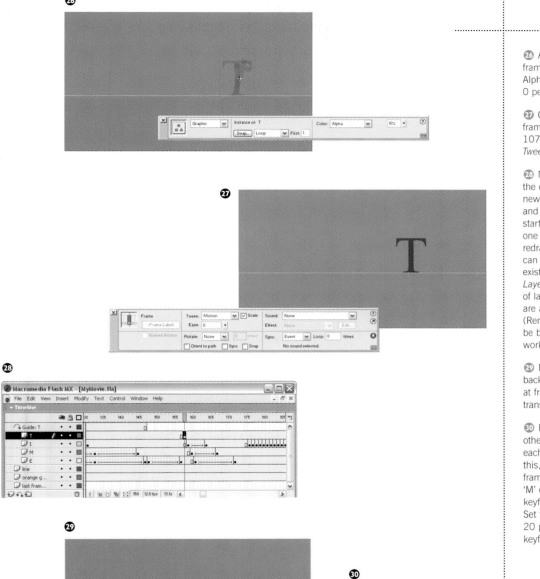

27

28

29

30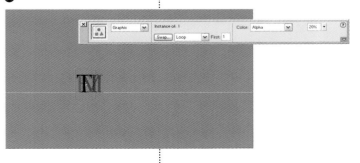

26 Add new keyframes at frames 65 and 119 and set the Alpha transparency to 10 and 0 per cent.

27 Click in the area between frames 65 and 79, and frames 107 and 119 and add *Motion Tweening* with default settings.

28 Now repeat the process for the other three letters. Add the new layers below the T layer and stagger each one so that it starts about 13 frames after the one before. You do not have to redraw the motion guide – you can attach each layer to the existing one by using *Modify > Layer > **Guided***. The names of layers attached to a guide are automatically indented. (Remember these layers must be below the guide layer to work.)

29 Now turn your attention back to layer T. Add a keyframe at frame 158 and set the Alpha transparency to 100 per cent.

30 Repeat the process with the other three letters and stagger each by a single frame. To do this, add a keyframe for 'I' on frame 159, add a keyframe for 'M' on frame 160 and add a keyframe for 'E' on frame 161. Set the Alpha transparency to 20 per cent for these three keyframes.

166

31 Now add yet another keyframe for each of these three layers; at frame 164 for 'I', 167 for 'M', and 172 for 'E'.

32 Move the three letters to the right so 'T I M E' is evenly spaced and centred in the width of the stage.

33 Set the Alpha transparency to 100 per cent for these three keyframes.

34 Click in the areas between keyframes 159–164, 160–167 and 161–172 and add *Motion Tweening*. The tweens get progressively longer as each letter has further to travel.

35 You now have 'T I M E' sitting static on the white line. In the next phase the letter 'I' will be replaced by rapidly changing numerals. So at frame 176 of layer 'I' add a keyframe. Use the Text tool to type the numeral '2', using Times New Roman selected from the *Character* panel at 120 point. Position it in exactly the same position as the 'I' it replaces on the timeline.

36 Keep adding keyframes and incrementally increasing the number, i.e. 2, 3, 4, 5, 6, 7, 8, 9, 0, and then return to 1 and repeat the process two more times. With no frames between them, the numbers will change at very high speed. It is not necessary to convert these to symbols since no tweening will be applied to them. Here, partial *Onion Skinning* shows the effect.

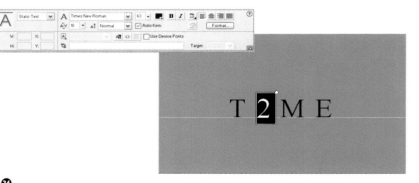

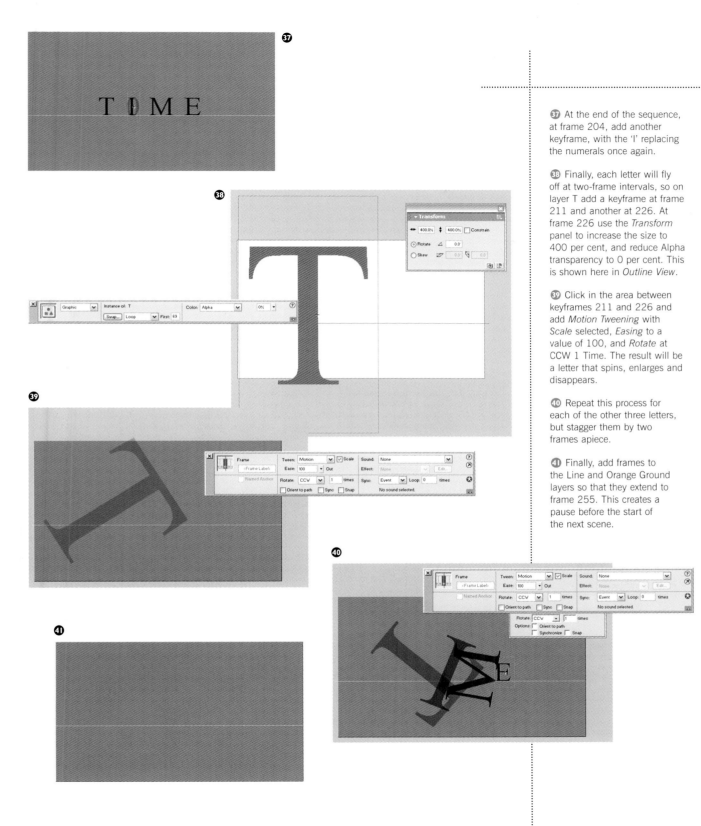

37 At the end of the sequence, at frame 204, add another keyframe, with the 'I' replacing the numerals once again.

38 Finally, each letter will fly off at two-frame intervals, so on layer T add a keyframe at frame 211 and another at 226. At frame 226 use the *Transform* panel to increase the size to 400 per cent, and reduce Alpha transparency to 0 per cent. This is shown here in *Outline View*.

39 Click in the area between keyframes 211 and 226 and add *Motion Tweening* with *Scale* selected, *Easing* to a value of 100, and *Rotate* at CCW 1 Time. The result will be a letter that spins, enlarges and disappears.

40 Repeat this process for each of the other three letters, but stagger them by two frames apiece.

41 Finally, add frames to the Line and Orange Ground layers so that they extend to frame 255. This creates a pause before the start of the next scene.

Scene 4: Birth

❶ Create a new layer named 'Orange Ground', and from *Library > General* drag onstage an Instance of the Variable Ground symbol. Position this using the Info panel by setting the x and y positions to 0, which will mean it covers the entire stage.

❷ Use the *Effects > Advanced* controls, or *Colour > Advanced* in Flash MX, to change the Instance colour to orange.

❸ Add a keyframe at frame 22 and change the Instance colour to green.

❹ Click in the area between keyframes 1 and 22 and add *Motion Tweening*. The colour changes from orange to green.

❺ Add a new layer named 'Line' and drag an instance of the Line symbol on stage. Position it exactly as it appears in the previous scene.

❻ Add a new keyframe at frame 29 and drag the Line just offstage at the bottom.

❼ Add *Motion Tweening* with default values.

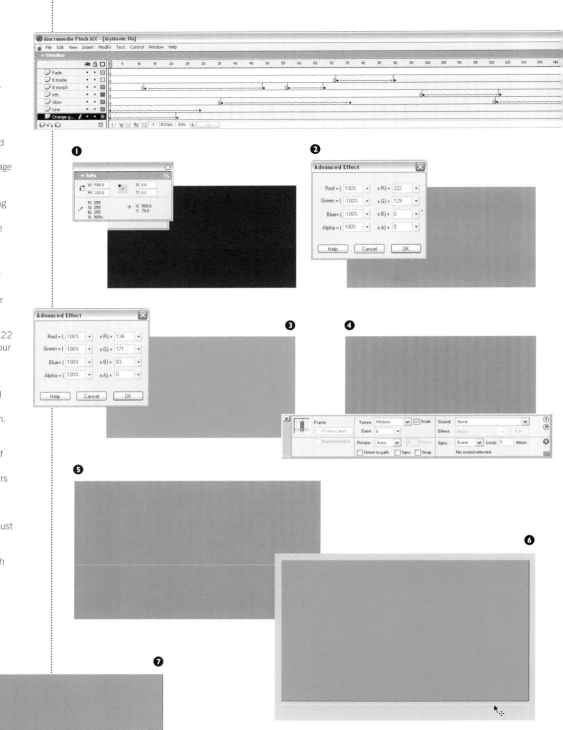

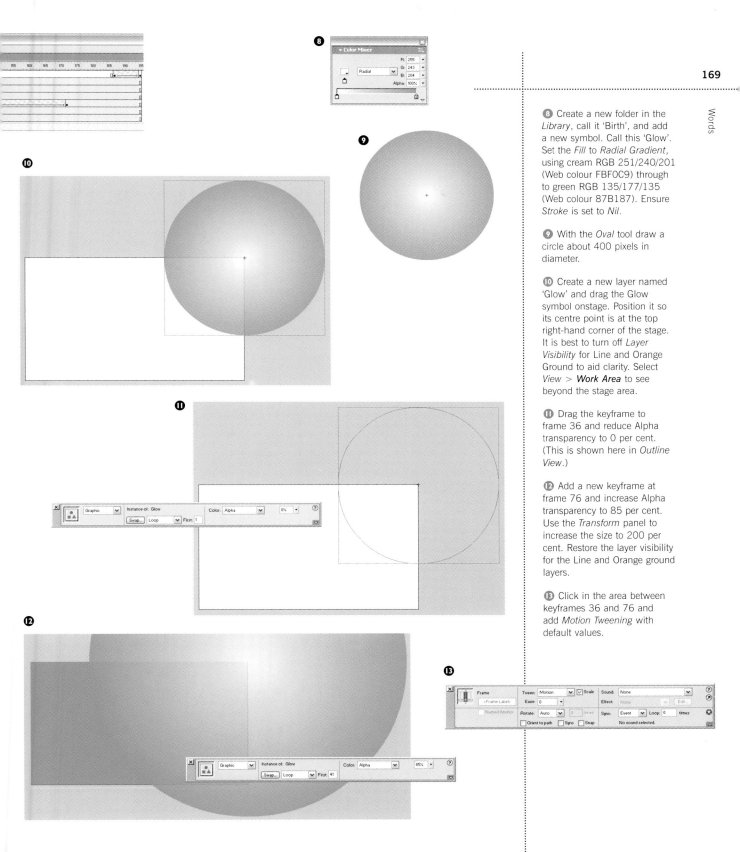

❽ Create a new folder in the *Library*, call it 'Birth', and add a new symbol. Call this 'Glow'. Set the *Fill* to *Radial Gradient*, using cream RGB 251/240/201 (Web colour FBF0C9) through to green RGB 135/177/135 (Web colour 87B187). Ensure *Stroke* is set to *Nil*.

❾ With the *Oval* tool draw a circle about 400 pixels in diameter.

❿ Create a new layer named 'Glow' and drag the Glow symbol onstage. Position it so its centre point is at the top right-hand corner of the stage. It is best to turn off *Layer Visibility* for Line and Orange Ground to aid clarity. Select *View* > **Work Area** to see beyond the stage area.

⓫ Drag the keyframe to frame 36 and reduce Alpha transparency to 0 per cent. (This is shown here in *Outline View*.)

⓬ Add a new keyframe at frame 76 and increase Alpha transparency to 85 per cent. Use the *Transform* panel to increase the size to 200 per cent. Restore the layer visibility for the Line and Orange ground layers.

⓭ Click in the area between keyframes 36 and 76 and add *Motion Tweening* with default values.

170

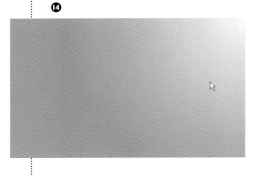

⓮ The background to this scene is now established, so next move onto the 'pregnant' letter B.

⓯ Create a new layer on the top and call it 'B Morph'. Use the *Text* tool to type the letter 'B' – try using Futura Light selected from the *Character* panel, making the text size 425 point. At this size the letter fills the full stage depth of 320 pixels, while an alternative font would need some size adjustment. Drag the keyframe to frame 57.

⓰ Use *Modify > **Break Apart*** to convert the text from a font into a graphic. The inside spaces of the B have to be removed so that the pregnant B shape can morph into the font-based letter B.

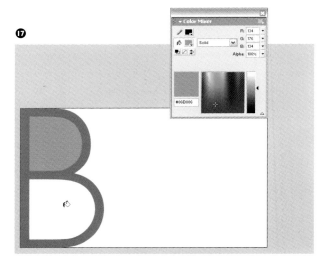

⓱ The inside spaces will be used again, so select them. At present they are empty, so fill them with green RGB 134/176/134 (Web colour 86B086).

⓲ Select these green shapes and create a new symbol named 'B Inside'. Then go to *Edit > **Paste in Place***.

⓳ Return to frame 57 of the B Morph layer and delete the green-filled shapes you've just created. Using the *Subselect* tool, proceed to delete the anchor points so that the interior shapes disappear altogether. (Other layers' visibility should be turned off for the sake of clarity.)

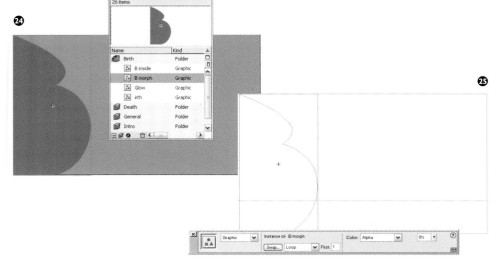

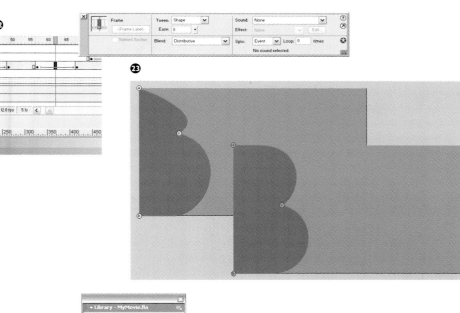

20 Add a keyframe at frame 68. Now restore the other layers' visibility.

21 Return to frame 57 and use the *Subselect* tool to reshape the B into the profile of a pregnant woman. This will be saved in the *Library* so that it can be reused, so copy the image and create a new symbol named 'B Morph' and select *Edit* > **Paste in Place**.

22 Click in the area between keyframes 57 and 68 and select *Frame* > *Shape* > **Tweening**. In Flash MX, choose *Tween* > **Shape** in the *Properties* window.

23 At frame 57 go to *Modify* > *Transform* > **Add Shape Hint**. (In Flash MX choose *Modify* > *Shape* > **Add Shape Hint**.) A small red letter 'a' will appear; drag that to the desired position, using maximum zoom. Then go to frame 68 and position the 'a' that has automatically appeared on this keyframe to the equivalent position on the altered letter, and repeat the process. When the *Shape Hints* are correctly positioned, they will change to yellow on the keyframe at the start of the tween, and green on the second one. Don't be alarmed if this takes a while to get right; it's a case of trial and error.

24 Insert two blank keyframes at frames 12 and 49. Drag another instance of the Symbol B morph onstage for each frame and position them exactly as you did on frame 57.

25 At keyframe 12 reduce Alpha transparency to 0 per cent. (This is best done in *Outline View* for clarity.)

172

26 Click in the area between keyframes 12 and 49 and add *Motion Tweening*.

27 Create a new layer named 'B Inside' above the others and add a blank keyframe at frame 72. Drag an instance of the Symbol B Inside onstage and position it above the B in the 'B Morph' layer so that it appears as a normal B again.

28 Reduce the Alpha transparency to 0 per cent.

29 At frame 90 add another blank keyframe and repeat the process described in the previous two steps, but this time set Alpha transparency to 100 per cent.

30 Click in the area between keyframes 72 and 90 and add *Motion Tweening*.

31 Create a new layer named 'irth' between the Glow and B Morph layers and add a new keyframe at frame 99. Use the *Text* tool to type the word 'irth' – try Futura Light from the *Character* panel, changing text size to 76 point and colour to purple RGB 137/109/160 (Web colour 896DA0). Position 'irth' so that it is partially obscured by the bottom bowl of the B. (This is best shown in *Outline View* for clarity.)

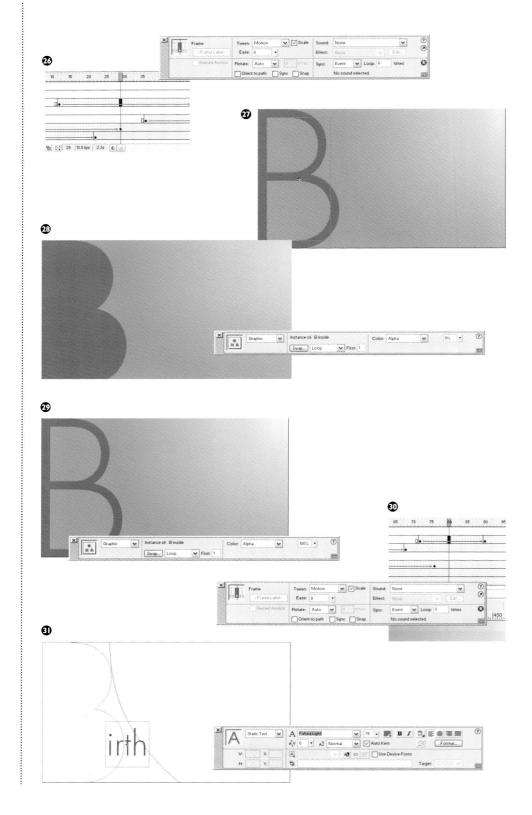

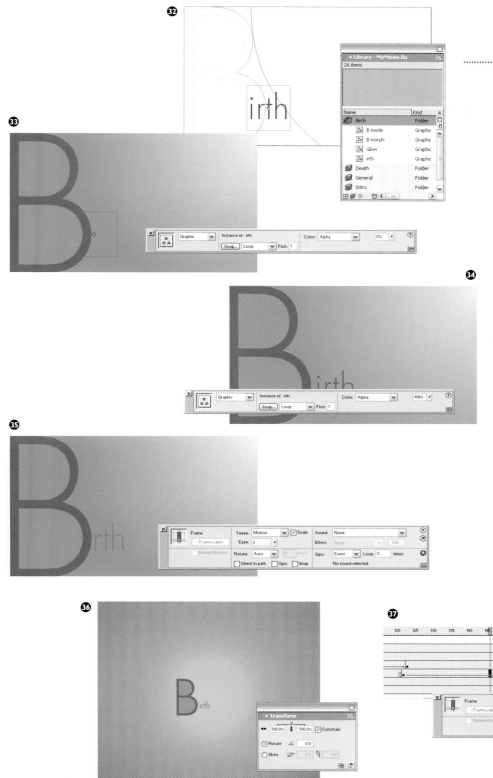

32 Select *Insert* > **Convert to Symbol** and name the new symbol 'irth'.

33 Reduce Alpha transparency to 0 per cent.

34 Add another keyframe at frame 123 and increase the Alpha transparency to 100 per cent.

35 Click in the area between keyframes 99 and 123 and add *Motion Tweening*.

36 Now return to the Glow layer and add new keyframes at frames 123 and 172. At frame 172 use the *Transform* panel to change the scaling to 700 per cent. Although in *Work Area View*, the full extent of the Glow image cannot be seen, as the *View Magnification* has been reduced to the minimum of 25 per cent.

37 Click in the area between keyframes 123 and 172 and add *Motion Tweening*.

38 At the end of this process, at frame 171, the animation looks like this.

You are nearly there now. The final part of this scene is a layer that provides a colour transition from the current scene to Scene 1. If you intend to add additional scenes, this layer may be different, and if you do not wish to loop the animation, it can be eliminated altogether.

39 Create a new layer named 'Fade' above the others. Add a keyframe at frame 187 and drag another instance of the Variable Ground symbol on stage. In the *Info* panel set both x and y to 0.

40 Use the *Effects* panel to change the *Colour* values to pale yellow and Alpha transparency to 0 per cent.

41 Add another keyframe at frame 195 and change the Alpha transparency to 100 per cent.

42 Click in the area between keyframes 187 and 195 and add *Motion Tweening*.

43 Finally, add frames to all the layers so that they finish at frame 195.

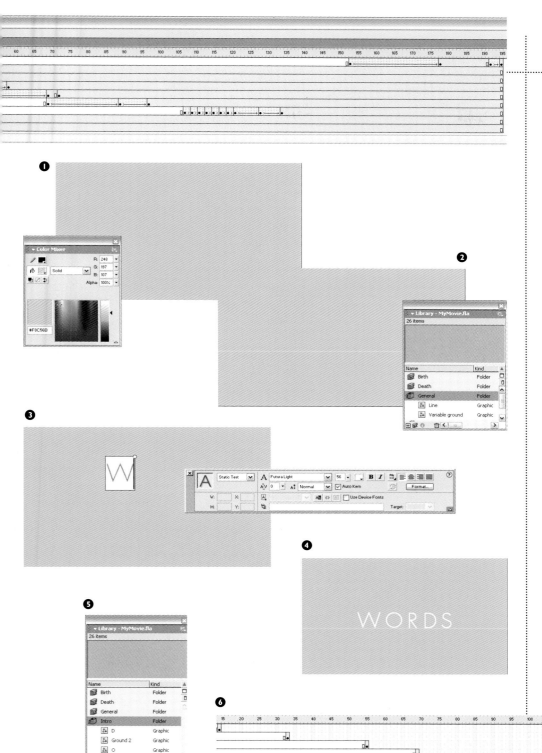

Scene 1: Intro

❶ Create a new layer called 'Orange Ground' for the background and fill it with the yellow RGB 248/197/107 (Web colour F8C56B) to match the final frame of scene 4. Convert this to a symbol and call it 'Ground 2'.

❷ Create a new layer named 'Line'. Drag another Instance of the *Line* symbol onstage. In the *Info* panel, set both x and y to 0. A white graphic will, of course, not be visible on the white *Library* background, so to see it change to *Outline View*.

❸ Create five new layers, one for each letter using Futura Light at 56 point. This font has an almost circular O, which enables it to 'bounce' like a ball. If you decide to use an alternative sans serif font, keep this in mind when choosing it.

❹ Position the five letters in their final location; keep plenty of space between them so that they do not touch their neighbour when animated.

❺ Convert each letter into a separate symbol.

❻ Drag the keyframe for each letter down the timeline so that the start positions are staggered – frames 14, 32, 55, 69 and 107 are the positions used in the example. Create another keyframe for each letter about 20 frames beyond the first. Don't worry about precise locations; all these frame positions can be adjusted as you try out the animation.

176

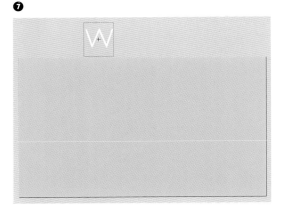

7 The position of the letters is the same for the two keyframes, so now drag the first one upwards beyond the stage, ensuring that *View > **Work Area*** is selected so that you can see the offstage area. It will be helpful to drag in a vertical guide to help with positioning.

8 Each letter will animate differently, so start work on the W. Click in the area between the two keyframes and go to *Frame > Effects > **Motion Tweening***, or *Tween > **Motion*** from the *Properties* window in Flash MX. Leave other options unselected except for *Scale*. (Although this is relevant only when the scale of an object changes, it does no harm to leave it permanently selected.) This letter rotates as it falls, so select CCW (anti/counter-clockwise) from the *Rotate* options and add 2 as the number of times.

9 Now for the letter O. Add three more keyframes between the existing two. All five are at the finish position, so select the first and move the letter up just offstage. The letter will now fall evenly between the first and second keyframes. The third keyframe shows the O being squashed as it hits the floor, so use *Modify > Transform > **Scale*** to reduce the vertical dimension – you should be able to judge this by eye.

10 Now click in the area between the second and third keyframes of O and apply *Motion Tweening* as you did for W, but this time adjust the *Easing* to 100. This will result in the tween beginning fast and slowing towards the end, just as a ball slows as it reaches the top of its bounce.

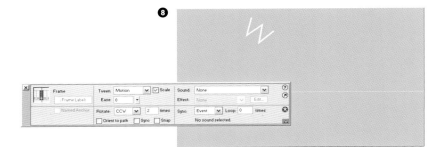

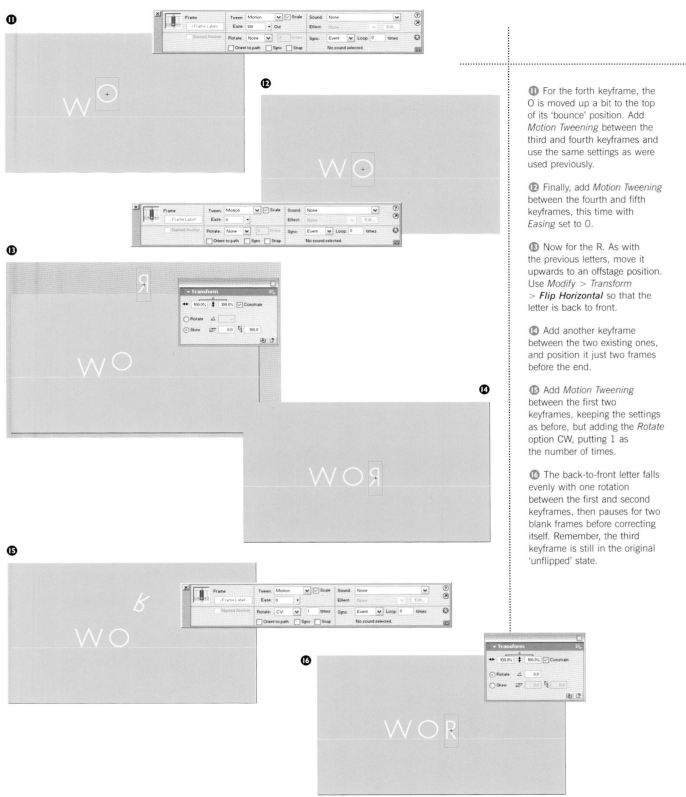

⓫ For the forth keyframe, the O is moved up a bit to the top of its 'bounce' position. Add *Motion Tweening* between the third and fourth keyframes and use the same settings as were used previously.

⓬ Finally, add *Motion Tweening* between the fourth and fifth keyframes, this time with *Easing* set to 0.

⓭ Now for the R. As with the previous letters, move it upwards to an offstage position. Use *Modify* > *Transform* > **Flip Horizontal** so that the letter is back to front.

⓮ Add another keyframe between the two existing ones, and position it just two frames before the end.

⓯ Add *Motion Tweening* between the first two keyframes, keeping the settings as before, but adding the *Rotate* option CW, putting 1 as the number of times.

⓰ The back-to-front letter falls evenly with one rotation between the first and second keyframes, then pauses for two blank frames before correcting itself. Remember, the third keyframe is still in the original 'unflipped' state.

⓱ Work on letter D next. Add another keyframe between the two already created and move the first upwards and offstage. Select the new keyframe and move the letter up to a midway position. Go to the *Transform* panel and set *Skew* to 20 degrees. You may have noticed that effects created using *Modify > Transform* are recorded in the *Transform* panel. Using either method can result in the same effect, although sometimes an effect is easier to apply using one method rather than the other.

⓲ Add *Motion Tweening* between the first and second frames, and between the second and third. Select *Frame > Effect > Rotate*, or the *Rotate* controls in Flash MX's *Properties* window, and set this to 3 times for both tweens. The effect is a frenetic gyration, which is in marked contrast to the other letters.

⓳ Finally, work on the letter S. The effect required here is to simulate the letter falling and rotating like a screw – it 'digs' itself into the 'ground' before popping back up again. Now move the letter at the first keyframe upwards and offstage, then add a further eight keyframes between the original two. There are now ten keyframes.

⓴ Move the second keyframe downwards and apply *Transform*.

㉑ Move the next keyframe downwards and apply *Transform*.

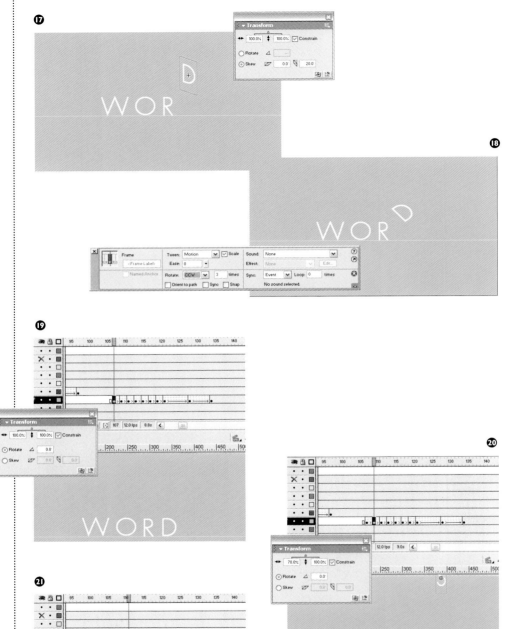

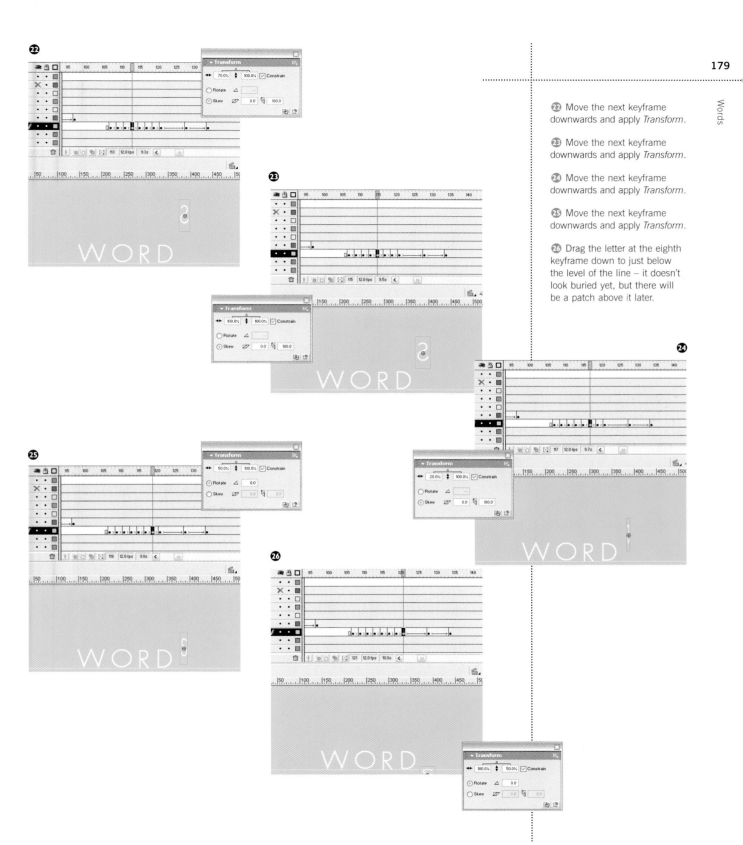

22 Move the next keyframe downwards and apply *Transform*.

23 Move the next keyframe downwards and apply *Transform*.

24 Move the next keyframe downwards and apply *Transform*.

25 Move the next keyframe downwards and apply *Transform*.

26 Drag the letter at the eighth keyframe down to just below the level of the line – it doesn't look buried yet, but there will be a patch above it later.

180

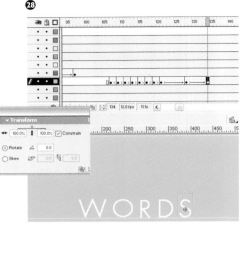

27 Next move the letter at the ninth keyframe to just above the line.

28 The tenth keyframe is already in the final position, sitting on the line.

29 Now add *Motion Tweening* between all ten frames using the default settings.

30 The *Onion Skin* view shows the five letters with all their tweened frames.

31 To complete scene 1, add a new layer named 'Patch for S' above the others. Use the *Rectangle* tool, with *Stroke* set to *Nil*, to create a yellow rectangle matching the background. This can be any size, as long as it covers the area below the line where the letter S dips beneath it. (Other layers can be hidden for clarity.)

32 Above that, add a new layer named 'Fade', which will provide the 'curtain' that draws across the screen and fades to match the next scene. Add a new keyframe at frame 153 and drag another Instance of the Variable Ground symbol onstage. In the *Info* panel, set both *x* and *y* to 0.

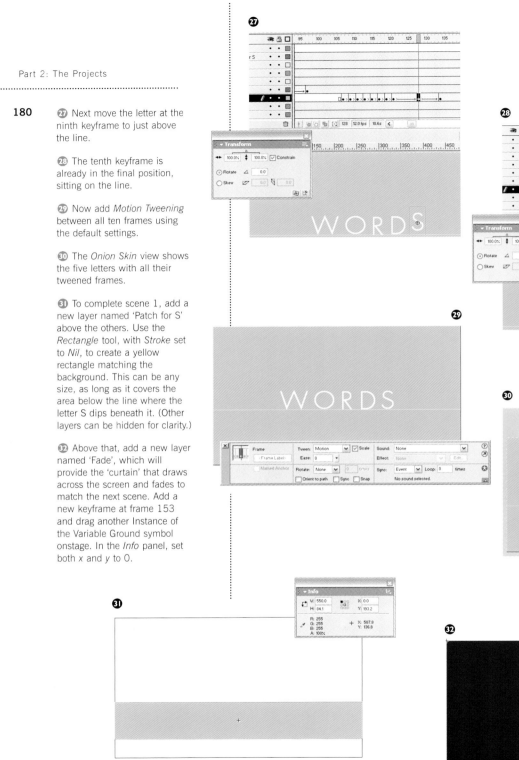

33

33 Reduce Alpha transparency to 0 per cent.

34 Add another keyframe at frame 178 and increase the Alpha transparency to 70 per cent.

35 Return to frame 153 and then drag the image partially offstage to the left.

36 Click in the area between keyframes 153 and 178 and add *Motion Tweening* with its default values.

37 Add keyframes at frame 192 and 195. At frame 195 increase Alpha transparency to 100 per cent. Click in the area between keyframes 192 and 195 and add *Motion Tweening*.

38 Finally add frames to all the layers so that they finish at frame 195.

34

35

36

37

38

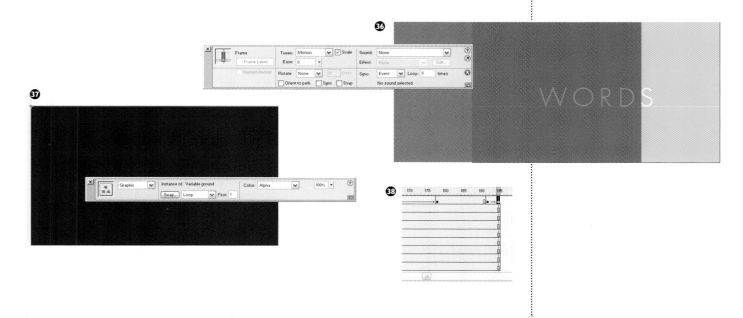

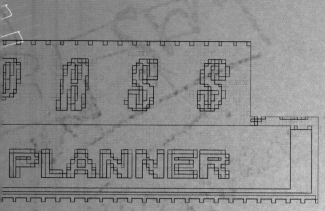

Reference

Glossary

3D Three dimensional – that is, an effect to give the illusion of depth on a flat page or monitor screen.

ADSL Asymmetric Digital Subscriber Line. Broadband telecommunication system, offering 'always on' Web access.

aliasing A term describing the jagged appearance of bitmapped images or fonts, either when the resolution is insufficient, or when they have been enlarged. This is caused by the pixels making up the image – which are square with straight sides – becoming visible.

animated GIF A GIF file containing more than one image. Many programs, including Web browsers, will display each of the images in turn, thus producing an animation. The delay between frames and the number of times the animation should loop can be specified in the file.

antialias/antialiasing A technique of optically eliminating the jagged effect of bitmapped images or text reproduced on low-resolution devices such as monitors. This is achieved by adding pixels of an in-between tone. The edges of the object's colour are blended with its background by averaging the density of the range of pixels involved. Antialiasing is also sometimes employed to filter texture maps, such as those used in 3D applications, to prevent moiré patterns.

background The area of an image on which the principal subject or foreground sits. It may be coloured to give extra definition to the image.

bandwidth The measure of the speed at which information is passed between two points, which may be between modems, across a 'bus', or from memory to disk. The broader the bandwidth, the faster data flows.

banner An image on a webpage, usually at the top, which deliberately attracts attention, generally for advertising purposes. Banner advertisements are often animated.

bit A contraction of 'binary digit', the smallest piece of information a computer can use. A bit is expressed as one of two values, 1 (on) or 0 (off).

bit depth The number of bits assigned to each pixel on a monitor, scanner or image file. One-bit, for example, will produce only black and white (the bit is either on or off), while 8-bit will generate 256 greys or colours (256 is the maximum number of permutations of a string of eight 1s and 0s), and 24-bit will produced 16.7 million colours (i.e. 256 x 256 x 256).

bitmap An array of values specifying the colour of every pixel in a digital image.

bitmapped graphic An image made up of dots, or pixels, and usually generated by 'paint' or 'image-editing' applications, as distinct from the 'vector' images of 'object-oriented' drawing applications.

browser An application enabling you to view, or 'browse', World Wide Web pages across the Internet.

button / navigation button A button in a Web browser, webpage or multimedia presentation that links you to a particular HTML page.

caption Any descriptive text that accompanies illustrative matter. It should, more accurately, be described as a legend.

Cartesian coordinate system A geometry system employed in any number of dimensions, from 2D upwards. It uses numbers to locate a point on a plane in relation to an origin where one or more points intersect.

cascading style sheet (CSS) A language defined by a World Wide Web Consortium recommendation for specifying the appearance (fonts, positioning, colour, etc.) of the elements of an HTML document.

cel In nondigital animation, a sheet of transparent acetate on which images for animation are drawn and painted. The traditional technique of cel animation is closely echoed in many digital animation applications, where animation is created on many different layers, and transparency is used to overlay the images.

clipping Limiting an image to within the bounds of a particular area.

clipping path An outline that defines which area of an image should be considered transparent or 'clipped'. This lets you isolate the foreground object, and is particularly useful when images are to be placed over new backgrounds.

CLUT Colour Look-up Table. A preset table of colours (to a maximum of 256) that the operating system uses when in 8-bit mode. CLUTS are also attached to individual images saved in 8-bit 'indexed' mode. When an application converts a 24-bit image (one with millions of colours) to 8-bit, it draws up a table ('index') of up to 256 colours. If a colour in the original image does not appear in the table, the application chooses the closest one or simulates it by 'dithering'.

colour depth This is the number of bits required to define the colour of each pixel. For example, only one bit is required to display a black-and-white image, while an 8-bit image can display either 256 greys or 256 colours, and a 24-bit image displays 16.7 million colours – eight bits each for red, green and blue (256 x 256 x 256).

compression The technique of rearranging data so that it either occupies less space on disk or transfers faster between devices or on communication lines. Compression methods that do not lose data are referred to as 'lossless', while 'lossy' describes methods in which some data is lost. There are many proprietary utilities for compressing data.

DHTML / Dynamic HTML A term loosely used to refer to the combination of JavaScript, cascading style sheets and basic HTML code, which enables you to add features including animation and rollover buttons to webpages, without relying on browser plug-ins or Java coding.

dial-up The term describing a connection to the Internet or to a network, which is made by dialling a telephone number for access and transferring data via a modem.

digital Anything operated by (or created from) information or signals represented by digits, such as in digital recording. As distinct from analog, in which information is represented by a physical variable.

digitize, digitalize To convert anything, such as text, images or sound, into binary (digital) form.

dither(ed), dithering A term referring to the use of patterns of pixels of available colours – for example, the colours in a 'Web-safe' palette – to simulate missing colours, based on the principle of optical mixing.

download To transfer data from a remote computer, such as an Internet server, to your own. The opposite of upload.

draw(ing) application Drawing applications can be defined as those that are object-oriented (they use 'vectors' to mathematically define lines and shapes), as distinct from painting applications, which use pixels to make images ('bitmapped graphics'). Some applications combine both.

drop shadow A shadow projected onto the background behind an image or character, designed to lift the image or character off the surface.

file format The way a program arranges data so that it can be stored or displayed on a computer. Common file formats are TIFF and JPEG for bitmapped image files, and EPS for object-oriented image files.

Flash (Macromedia) Software for creating vector graphics and animations for Web presentations. Flash generates small files, which are correspondingly quick to download and, being vector, are scalable to any dimension.

fps Frames per second. The units in which frame-rate is most often specified.

frame (1) In animation, a single, still image that is part of an animated sequence.

frame (2) On the Web, also a means of displaying more than one page at a time within a single window. A common use of frames is to display a menu that remains static while other parts of the webpage – displayed in the same window – contain information that can be 'scrolled'.

frame rate The speed at which the individual frames of an animation are substituted for one another; that is, the speed at which the animation is played. This rate is usually specified as a number of frames per second, but may be indicated in another way, for example, by delay between the substitution of frames, expressed in hundredths of a second, in animated GIFs.

GIF Graphics Interchange Format. One of the main bitmapped image formats used on the Internet. Devised by CompuServe (now part of AOL), GIF is a 256-colour format with two specifications, GIF87a and, more recently, GIF89a, the latter providing additional features such as transparent

186 backgrounds. The GIF format uses a 'lossless' compression technique, or algorithm, that does not squeeze files as much as the JPEG format, which is 'lossy' (some data is lost). For use in Web browsers, JPEG is the format of choice for tone images, such as photographs, while GIF is more suitable for line images and other graphics.

Gourand shading A method of rendering by manipulating colours and shades selectively along the lines of certain vertices, which are then averaged across each polygon face in order to create a realistic light and shade effect.

greyscale The rendering of an image, either fore- or background, in a range of greys from white to black. In a digital image and on a computer monitor, this usually means that an image is rendered with eight bits assigned to each pixel, giving a maximum of 256 levels of grey.

HTML Hypertext Markup Language. A text-based 'page description language' (PDL) used to format documents published on the World Wide Web, which can be viewed with Web browsers.

image slicing The practice of dividing up a single digital image into rectangular areas, which can then each, for example, be optimized separately or have different links attached to them. On a website, though, visitors still see the original, single image, and are unaware of the slices.

indexed colour An image mode of a maximum of 256 colours that is used in some applications, such as Adobe Photoshop, to reduce the file size of RGB images, so that they can be used in, for example, multimedia presentations or webpages. This is achieved by using an indexed table of colours (a colour look-up table, or CLUT).

interactive animation Animation that varies, develops or responds as a direct result of some user input, such as a mouse or keyboard event.

interface / user interface The facilities for interaction that a computer program presents to its human users – for example, the desktop interface to an operating system.

interpolation A computer calculation used to estimate unknown values that fall between known ones. One use of this process is to redefine pixels in bitmapped images after they have been modified in some way – for instance, when an image is resized (called 'resampling') or rotated, or if colour corrections have been made. In such cases the program takes estimates from the known values of other pixels lying in the same or similar ranges. Interpolation is also used by some scanning and image-manipulation software to enhance the resolution of images that have been scanned at low resolution.

inverse kinematics A method of animating structures that form a chain of links, such as a human arm. The position of all the elements in the chain – for example, forearm, elbow, upper arm, etc., are computed to fit the position of the final element.

ISDN Integrated Services Digital Network. Telecommunication technology that transmits data on special digital lines rather than on analog lines.

ISP Internet Service Provider. Any organisation that provides access to the Internet. At its most basic this may merely be a telephone number for connection, but most ISPs also provide e-mail addresses and capacity for your own webpages.

Java A programming language originally designed by Sun MicroSystems for the control of household appliances, which is especially suited for Internet use because it can run on any platform. Java programs can be turned into applets (small applications), which can be efficiently transmitted over the Internet to run in a user's browser. Java is thus a useful and powerful tool for interactive animation.

JavaScript A 'scripting' language for applying dynamic effects to webpages.

JPEG / JPG Joint Photographics Experts Group. An ISO (International Standards Organization) group that defines compression standards for bitmapped colour images. The abbreviated form, pronounced 'jay-peg', gives its name to a 'lossy' (some data may be lost) compressed file format in which the degree of compression from high compression/low quality to low compression/high quality can be user defined.

key frame (1) In traditional animation the key drawings or 'extremes' show the position of characters, etc., at the start and finish of a movement or action. These key drawings are done first, and then the in-between drawings are created to complete the illusion of a smooth or effective movement. This concept has been transferred to digital animation and motion graphics in the form of key frames. A key frame is thus a frame whose contents are fully specified (either by drawing or other image creation, and/or by the setting of precise parameters), as opposed to those frames that are interpolated – or tweened – by computation.

key frame (2) A single animation frame in a QuickTime sequence in which information is stored as a reference so that subsequent frames store only changes in the frame ('differences'), rather than storing the whole frame each time, thus making the file smaller. The frames based on changes are called 'delta frames' or 'difference frames'.

keyline A line drawing indicating the size and position of an illustration in a layout.

lossless compression Methods of file compression in which no data is lost (as opposed to lossy compression).

lossy compression Methods of file compression in which some data may be irretrievably lost during compression (as opposed to lossless compression). JPEG is a lossy-compression format.

LZW (Lempel-Ziv-Welch) A widely supported lossless-compression method for bitmapped images. It gives a compression ratio of 2:1 or more, depending on the range of colours in an image.

Mbps Megabits per second. A measure of data transfer speeds. A megabit is 1024 kilobits.

menu A display on a computer screen showing the list of choices available to a user.

midtones/middletones The range of tonal values in an image anywhere between the darkest and lightest, usually referring to those approximately halfway.

mouse event Any input from the mouse occurring at a distinct point in time. Mouse events include pressing and releasing the mouse button.

mouse-over The mouse event that occurs when the mouse pointer rolls over a navigation button.

MPEG The Moving Picture Experts Group is in charge of the development of standards for the coded representation of

digital audio and video. Established in 1988, the group produced MPEG-1, the standard on which video CD and MP3 are based; MPEG-2, the standard on which digital television set-top boxes and DVD are based; and MPEG-4, the standard for multimedia on the Web. The current thrust is MPEG-7, 'Multimedia Content Description Interface'. Work on the new standard MPEG-21, 'Multimedia Framework', started in June 2000.

navigation bar A special bar in a Web browser, webpage or multimedia presentation designed to help you to 'navigate' through pages by clicking on buttons or text.

online Any activity taking place on a computer or device while it is connected to a network such as the Internet. The opposite of offline.

operating system The software (and in some cases 'firmware') that provides the environment within which all other software and its user operates. The major operating systems are Microsoft's 'DOS' and 'Windows', Apple's 'Mac OS' and AT&T's 'UNIX', the last three of which all use 'GUIs' (graphical user interfaces).

packet A bundle of data, the basic unit transmitted across networks. When data is sent over a network such as the Internet, it is broken up into small chunks called packets, which are sent independently of each other.

paint(ing) applications Applications that use bitmaps of pixels to create images rather than the 'vectors' that describe lines in drawing applications (called 'object-oriented'). Some applications combine both.

parallax The apparent movement of two objects relative to each other when viewed from different positions.

perspective A technique of rendering three-dimensional objects on a two-dimensional plane, duplicating the 'real world' view by giving the same impression of the object's relative position and size when viewed from a particular point. The shorter the distance, the wider the perspective; the greater the distance, the narrower the perspective.

pixel Short for 'picture element'. The smallest component of any digitally generated image, including text, such as a single dot of light on a computer screen. In its simplest form, one pixel corresponds to a single bit: 0 = off, or white, and

188 1 = on, or black. In colour or greyscale images or monitors, one pixel may correspond to up to several bits. An 8-bit pixel, for example, can be displayed in any of 256 colours (the total number of different configurations that can be achieved by eight 0s and 1s).

pixelation/pixellization The term used to describe an image that has been broken up into square blocks resembling pixels, giving it a 'digitized' look.

plug-in Software, which is usually developed by a third party in order to extend the capabilities of another particular piece of software. Plug-ins are common in image-editing and page-layout applications for such things as special-effect filters. Plug-ins are also common in Web browsers for such features as playing movies and audio.

PNG Portable Network Graphics. A file format for images used on the Web that provides 10–30% 'lossless' compression, and supports variable transparency through 'Alpha channels', cross-platform control of image brightness, and interlacing.

progressive JPEG A digital image format used primarily for displaying JPEG images on webpages. The image is displayed in progressively increasing resolutions as the data is downloaded to the browser. A cloudy image appears on the screen, which clears as more data is downloaded. Also called 'proJPEG'.

QuickTime Apple's software program and system extension that enables computers running either Windows or the Mac OS to play film and sound files, particularly over the Internet and in multimedia applications, providing cut, copy and paste features for moving images and automatic compression and decompression of image files.

QuickTimeVR QuickTime 'virtual reality'. An Apple extension that provides features for the creation and playback of 3D objects or panoramic scenes.

rasterize(d) To rasterize is to electronically convert a vector graphics image into a bitmapped image. This may introduce aliasing, but is often necessary when preparing images for the Web; without a plug-in, browsers can only display GIF, JPEG and PNG image files.

raytracing A rendering algorithm that simulates the physical and optical properties of light rays as they reflect off a 3D model, thus producing realistic shadows and reflections.

RealVideo Proprietary streaming video format widely used on the Web, which depends on a plug-in in the user's browser to work.

resolution (1) The degree of quality, definition or clarity with which an image is reproduced or displayed in – for example, – a photograph, or via a scanner, monitor, printer or other output device.

resolution (2): monitor resolution, screen resolution The number of pixels across by pixels down. The three most common resolutions are 640 x 480, 800 x 600, and 1024 x 768. The current standard Web page size is 800 x 600.

RGB Short for 'Red, green, blue': the colours of the 'additive' colour model.

rollover The rapid substitution of one or more images when the mouse pointer is rolled over the original image. Used extensively for navigation buttons on webpages and multimedia presentations.

shareware Software available through user groups, magazine cover disks, etc., which is usually paid for only by those users who decide to continue using it. Although shareware is not 'copy protected', it is protected by copyright and a fee is normally payable for using it, unlike 'freeware'.

Shocked The term applied to webpages that contain material prepared with Macromedia's Shockwave technology, and therefore require the Shockwave plug-in to be viewed.

Shockwave A technology developed by Macromedia for creating Director (video) presentations, which can be delivered over the Internet and viewed with a Web browser.

sprite In animation, a sprite is an object or character that is animated by the substitution of a different image or sprite face for each state, such as the different positions of a waving arm, and the adjustment of its position on the screen. This technique is used widely in animation controlled by computer programming; for example, in Java animation.

stop-motion A term often used to refer to the creation of animation by the process of taking a sequence of photographs (on film, video tape or direct to disk) of static 3D characters and sets that are slightly moved or altered between frames in order to create an illusion of motion when played back in sequence.

storyboard A series of small drawings representing key moments, movements and changes in a live-action film or animation, which are laid out in sequence like a comic strip in order to convey a sense of the narrative or development of the piece. The drawings are usually accompanied by captions describing the action and sound.

streaming video/audio A method of transmitting video or audio that allows it to be played continuously and apparently in real time. Segments of the received data are buffered while the user's software plays the previous buffered section.

SVG Scalable Vector Graphics. A vector graphics format devised for use on the Web, defined by a World Wide Web Consortium recommendation. SVG images are compact compared with bitmaps, and can be displayed at any size and resolution without loss of quality.

TIFF, TIF Tagged Image File Format. A standard and popular graphics file format originally developed by Aldus (now merged with Adobe) and Microsoft, used for scanned, high-resolution, bitmapped images and for colour separations. The TIFF format can be used for black-and-white, greyscale and colour images, which have been generated on different computer platforms.

tile, tiling Repeating a graphic item and placing the repetitions side-by-side in all directions so that they form a pattern, or a continuous background.

tween(ing) A contraction of 'in-between'. An animator's term for the process of creating transitional frames to fill in-between key frames in an animation.

twenty-four-bit/24-bit colour The allocation of 24 bits of memory to each pixel, giving a possible screen display of 16.7 million colours (a row of 24 bits can be written in 16.7 million different combinations of 0s and 1s). Twenty-four bits are required for CMYK separations – eight bits for each.

URL Uniform Resource Locator. The unique address of a page on the Web, comprising three elements: the protocol to be used (such as http), the domain name ('host'), and the directory name followed by path-names to any particular file.

vector graphics Images made up of mathematically defined shapes, such as circles and rectangles, or complex paths built out of mathematically defined curves. Vector graphics images can be displayed at any size or resolution without loss of quality, and are easy to edit because the shapes retain their identity, but they lack the tonal subtlety of bitmapped images. Because vector graphics files are typically small, they are well suited to Web animation.

visualization The representation of complex data and information in an easily grasped visual form – for example, an animation showing the evolution of a tropical storm, where wind speed is represented by colour.

VRML Virtual Reality Modelling Language. An HTML-type programming language designed to create 3D scenes.

website The address, location (on a server) and collection of documents and resources for any particular interlinked set of web pages.

window Part of the 'graphical user interface' (GUI) of a computer, a window is an area of a computer screen that displays the contents of disk, folder or document. A window can be resized and is scrollable if the contents are too large to fit within it.

Windows Media (Player) A Microsoft multimedia format widely used for Web video.

wizard A help facility that guides users through tasks, such as software installation or the use of a Java applet.

World Wide Web (WWW) The term given to describe the entire collection of webpages all over the world connected to the Internet. The term also describes the particular type of Internet access architecture that uses a combination of HTML and various graphic formats, such as GIF and JPEG, to publish formatted text, which can be read by browsers.

World Wide Web Consortium (W3C) The organisation jointly responsible for managing standards across the Web.

z-order(ing) The stacking order of layers (from front to back) in a program such as Photoshop, or objects in a three-dimensional scene.

Index

Bold indicates a glossary entry

Useful Websites

Fonts

www.getfonts.com/fonts/category/Cool/
http://members.tripod.com/~bhaavana/embedded/faq.html#10
www.fontsite.com/home.html
www.makambo.com/fonts/found.jsp?foundryid=
    111&affiliateid=031450
www.bitstream.com/index.html
www.microsoft.com/typography/default.asp
www.fontbureau.com/cgi-bin/index.cgi
www.microsoft.com/typography/web/embedding/
    weft/default.htm
www.adobe.com/type/opentype/main.html
http://freetype.sourceforge.net/freetype2/docs/glyphs/
    index.html

Music and Sound

http://listen.to/midipalace
www.cowdance.com/frame.html
www.tvtrecords.com/
www.ldg.be/

Animation

www.virtual-fx.net/
www.macromedia.com/support/flash/
http://animation.about.com/arts/animation/library/weekly/
    blflashtutorial2b.htm

www.macromedia.com/support/flash/interactivity/
    smart_preloader/
www.macromedia.com/solutions/richmedia/
www.hyperquake.com/
www.macromedia.com/exchange/flash/
http://forums.ultrashock.com/ff.htm?forums.ultrashock.
    com/forums203/index.php?s=
www.flashmagazine.com/flash4.htm
http://web.inter.nl.net/users/anima/index.htm
www.flashkit.com/
www.swishportal.com/links.htm
http://surface.yugop.com/
www.erain.com/
www.flashmove.com/
www.howstuffworks.com/at-0.htm
www.shockwave.com/bin/shockwave/entry.jsp
www.totallyhip.com/lo/index.html
http://graphicssoft.about.com/library/weekly/aa000713a.htm
http://atomfilms.shockwave.com/af/home/
www.xaraxone.com/index.htm
http://animation.about.com/
www.loonyverse.com/shockwave.html

Browser

http://preciousbundles.com/wd4cbc/
www.dansteinman.com/dynduo/